more than a story

"In *More Than a Story*, Scott weaves the lyrics to his songs into the lyrics to our lives. I enjoyed learning the stories behind the songs, but I was blessed even more with a deeper love and understanding for the words of God that inspired the songs Scott sings. This book will touch everyone who reads it in a special way."
—**Debbie Trafton O'Neal,** Author, *Family Time* and *Family Fun*

"In a world where it's hard to know who to trust, *More Than a Story* takes an honest, practical, fresh look at living the Christian life—day-by-day, minute-by-minute. I know Scott Krippayne's heart for God and his love for kids, and I can't wait for my kids to get their hands on this book."
—**Mark DeVries,** Youth Pastor, First Presbyterian Church, Nashville, Tennessee
Author, *Family-Based Youth Ministry*

"You will not only be blessed, you will be challenged by Scott's daily devotionals. He writes straight from his heart, with thought-provoking questions and fresh insights into God's Word. If you want to enhance your daily time with Christ, I highly recommend *More Than a Story.*"
—**Shelley Breen,** Point of Grace

"In Scott's new book of daily reflections, he has skillfully woven together lyrics, Scripture, questions, life experiences, and great insights into one great book. I highly recommend *More Than a Story.*"
—**Denny Rydberg,** President, YoungLife

"*More Than a Story* reveals what I already knew to be true about Scott Krippayne: he has a practical spirituality, an energetic approach to life, deep personal loyalties, and a genuine love for Christ. Scott's book of devotionals verifies his Christ-like attitude toward life."
—**Elwyn Raymer,** Vice President, BMG Music Publishing

"This book allowed me a closer look at the practical and powerful scriptural applications contained in Scott's lyrics. I have no doubt that people will be drawn closer to Jesus through this book."
—**Charlie Peacock,** Director, A&R, re:think and
Multiple Award Winning Producer

more than a story
a daily touch of the Savior's love

scott krippayne

HOWARD
PUBLISHING CO.

THE ARTISTS DEVOTIONAL SERIES

Our purpose at Howard Publishing is to:

- *Increase faith* in the hearts of growing Christians
- *Inspire holiness* in the lives of believers
- *Instill hope* in the hearts of struggling people
  everywhere

Because He's coming again!

More Than a Story © 1998 by Scott Krippayne
All rights reserved. Printed in the United States of America

Published by Howard Publishing Co., Inc.,
3117 North 7th Street, West Monroe, Louisiana 71291-2227

98 99 00 01 02 03 04 05 06 07   10 9 8 7 6 5 4 3 2 1

Library of Congress Cataloging-in Publication Data
Krippayne, Scott, 1970–
    More than a story : a daily touch of the Savior's love / Scott Krippayne
      p.   cm. — (The artists devotional series)
      ISBN 1-878990-83-7
      1. Meditations. 2. Contemporary Christian music—Texts.
    I. Krippayne, Scott, 1970- Songs. Texts. Selections. II. Title.
    III. Series.
    BV4832.2.K73 1998
    242—dc21   98-9700
                                                            CIP

Interior design by LinDee Loveland
Manuscript editing by Traci Mullins

■ DEDICATION

to everyone God has used in my life to plant seeds,
share the Gospel, and strengthen my faith.
You changed the world for me,
and I am eternally grateful.

■ CONTENTS

contents

■ ACKNOWLEDGMENTS

I would like to thank:
My heavenly Father—for sending your Son, loving us perfectly and loving faithfully
My wonderful wife Katy—for your unending encouragement and support. I'm grateful for the years we've had together and look forward to the years to come. I love you.
Everyone at Howard Publishing—for the opportunity to dive deeper into the songs and my own faith
Gary Myers—for your courage and friendship
Philis Boultinghouse—you're amazing and gifted. I never thought the editing process would be so enjoyable.
Mike Atkins—for your wisdom and perseverance
The songwriters—for sharing your heart

introduction

Questions. I'm intrigued by them. I'm drawn to people who ask good ones. I ask a few myself. Questions. I like the ones that make me think a little—the kind that don't always have easy answers: Is God real? What's he like? What does that mean for me?

When I was a kid in school, I hardly ever raised my hand to ask a question, for fear it might be dumb. But now I'm not so sure that any of them are dumb. Questions help us define what we believe. I like questions that rock my world, or at least rattle it a bit. How are my relationships doing? Why do I do what I do? Why on earth am I writing a book? Now there's a good one.

I've written songs for a number of years; it's been a way to communicate. Music allows me to pour out my heart and frame my thoughts. But why write a book? Well, I guess it's a way to dive a little deeper into the things I'm passionate about, to share a bit more of my heart, and to ask some more questions. And of course, a book doesn't have to rhyme.

Through this book, I will explore the ideas and concepts of a few songs more thoroughly and give you a peek at some of the questions I'm wrestling with and how God is a part of it all. And if my hunch is right, you're asking some of the same questions I am. My prayer is that this book will move both of us a little farther along in our journies of faith, that we become more aware that what we read in our Bibles is much more than a story, and that the words we share together will put us in touch daily with the Savior's love.

Scott

1

more

ore
more

i used to read about a man
who could walk across the sea
they say He fed five thousand people
and died to set us free
then Your love removed the veil from my eyes
and after all these years i finally realized—You are . . .

(Chorus)
more than a story written on a page
more than a feeling deep inside
You are more than a spirit spinning out in space
not who i thought You were before
You are so much more

when i think i've got You down
You move a different way
and You remind me once again
there are still things i can't explain
because You're the one who set the moon and stars in place
but someday i will get to see You face to face—'cause You are . . .

(Chorus)

You are my Savior, my Redeemer, and my friend
You walked this earth before
and You're coming back again
You're the Almighty King of kings and Lord of lords
Creator of all things and so much more—You are . . .

(Chorus)

You are the way, You are the truth, You are the life
and i believe that You're alive

Scott Krippayne, Tony Miracle and Charlie Peacock
© 1996 BMG Songs, Inc. (ASCAP), Above The Rim Music (ASCAP), Meadowgreen Music/
Sugar Pete Songs (ASCAP) and Sparrow Songs/Andi Beat Goes On (BMI). All rights on behalf
of Above The Rim Music administered by BMG Songs, Inc. (ASCAP)

"More" began as a musical idea—pure and simple. Tony, Charlie, and I sat down in the studio, pounded out some chords, and wrote a melody. And at that point, the real work began—the lyric.

We had already chosen a number of songs for the record, but there were still a few things I felt I needed to say. I remembered a conversation I'd had with a young lady after a concert. She told me she felt as if God were just beyond her reach. She couldn't quite grasp who he was, and she had a hard time believing he could really love her. It broke my heart. I reflected back on the time in my life when God seemed far away, when I wondered if he could hear me—or if he even wanted to. I thought of the times I had spent in his Word without seeing beyond the words on the page. It's easy to lose sight of an invisible God. How do you explain to someone that God is real? How do you remind yourself?

It was questions and experiences like those that helped lead to the lyric of "More." God is far greater than we can comprehend, but we must hold on to the things we do understand. The lyrics in the bridge are my favorite part; sometimes I get chills when I sing them. There's something powerful about saying the names of God out loud. If nothing else, they serve as a reminder that he is alive, well, and at work.

more

What was Jesus thinking about as he was stretched out on the cross?

- God demonstrates his own love for us in this: While we were still sinners, Christ died for us.

  Romans 5:8

more than a story

"Scott Andrew-ew-ew" my mom called. "Your father's got the car running. It's time to go." It was Sunday morning—time to head off to church, time to sit quietly, sing a little, and try to listen. I didn't mind it much. We went together as a family, and by the time we got home, a football game was usually about to start.

I grew up going to church every single Sunday. I went; I endured; I went home. I learned some things *about* God, but I never really got to know *him*. I heard Bible stories, but I thought they were just that—stories. I never dreamed that the people might be real. I'd hear about Jesus walking on the water or feeding five thousand people with only five loaves of bread and two fish, and I'd think, "Cool—nice story."

Over the years, as you might imagine, I heard a lot of "nice stories." But when I was seventeen, something changed. I met Jesus. He was real. God was real. The stories I had heard for so many years began to make sense. I realized that the Bible wasn't just a collection of stories—it was actually the *Word of God*. The stories were true. God did speak to Moses though a burning bush. David really did fight Goliath and win. Peter actually walked on water. Adam and Abraham, Job and Jonah, Matthew, Mark, Luke, and John—they all walked this same earth many years ago. And Jesus: His miracles happened. His words were heard. His death was real. And his grave was empty. The stories of the Bible and the lives recorded there are windows through which we may see a real God.

I met Jesus ten years ago, but every so often I find myself just reading stories again. I'll sit down, open up the Bible, read an amazing story, and forget that the word *God* speaks of the God I pray to and that the name *Jesus* is the name of the Son of God who gave up his life for mine. Sometimes I miss the reality.

Imagine what it would have been like to live in biblical times . . . to hear Abraham tell you that his wife was expecting a child or David tell of his battle with Goliath. Or put yourself in the shoes of some of the people you read about. What was it like for the blind man to be given his sight? What was it like for Paul to lose his on the road to Damascus? What was going through Noah's mind when the water finally subsided and he stepped out of the ark onto dry land? And what was Jesus thinking about as he was stretched out on the cross? It's amazing what a fresh perspective can do.

Our God is so much more than just a collection of stories. But through the stories, we can come to know him better. We can see how he worked in the lives of those who lived hundreds of years ago. We can see his perfect plan working out through the centuries. And we can have a relationship with a living God who loves us more than we can imagine.

questions to ponder . . .

1. Are you getting to know God himself or just learning about him?

2. How can you get to know him better?

3. What story is God unfolding in your life now?

4. What is he trying to show you or teach you?

5. In what ways are the stories of the Bible your own story?

time in prayer . . .

Thank God for his Word and for the ways he reveals himself. Thank him for the opportunity to have a relationship with him. Ask the Lord to help you get to know him better and learn more about his ways.

Why now, God?

■ "For my thoughts are not your thoughts, neither
are your ways my ways," declares the Lord. "As
the heavens are higher than the earth, so are my
ways higher than your ways and my thoughts than
your thoughts."

Isaiah 55:8–9

not our ways

It was August 1, 1993, and I was preparing to move. I had started the process of packing, saying goodbye to close friends, and wrapping up twenty-three wonderful years in Seattle, Washington. This chapter of my life was nearing a close, and I was excited about beginning the next one. I was on my way to Nashville, Tennessee, to continue my growth as a songwriter. I had been praying for months and felt a real peace about the move. The timing seemed perfect: my parents had left for Arizona, I had recently graduated from college, and I was single. All signs pointed go.

How was I supposed to know that on the afternoon of August 1, I would meet *her?* This couldn't be right. *Why now, God?* I thought. *This isn't part of "our" plan!* I was supposed to leave Seattle with no strings attached. I thought God and I had this all figured out. Apparently, he had different ideas. Katy and I spent the next two and a-half months getting to know each other, and I soon realized I would have a large long-distance phone bill in Tennessee. I went ahead with the move in October, and Katy and I continued to grow closer across the miles.

We were married on July 29, 1994. I am so thankful God had a different plan from mine. My plan didn't account for Katy, but God knew. He knew what he was doing the whole time. I didn't understand it at first and was even pretty resistant—"God, I didn't want to meet someone *now!*"—but I eventually realized that God was looking at a much bigger picture. Once again, the Lord knew what was best. Katy is an amazing, wonderful, and precious gift.

God's ways are different from ours. When I think I've got things figured out, he surprises me with something better. Sometimes I try to put God in a box so I can understand him, but he never fits. He is far beyond my comprehension. He looks at, sees, and does things differently than we do. God's ways are higher than our ways. Look how he's surprised us throughout the ages.

- He promised Abraham, who was nearly one hundred years old, that he would have off spring as numerous as the stars and be the father of many nations. (Genesis 15:3–5; 17:3–6)

- He used Peter, who denied Christ three times, as the rock on which he built his church. (Matthew 16:18)

- He made Paul, who had threatened and persecuted many Christians, a powerful missionary for Christ. (Acts 22:4–15)

- And God's Son, Jesus, King of kings, Lord of lords, and Savior of the world, was born in a manger and died on a cross. (Luke 2:4–7; John 19:16–18, 28–30)

What is God's plan for your life? As you look back over the years, have things always worked out the way you thought they would? In what ways has God surprised you? What are your plans for the future? Where do you think the Lord wants to take you? Whatever the answers to these questions may be, God has been, is, and will be in control.

God's way is most assuredly the best way. I've seen it time and time again in his Word, and I've seen it in my own life. The one who created the moon and the stars had a plan then, and he has a plan now.

questions to ponder . . .

1. Do you ever try to put God in a box? In what ways?

2. Has he broken out of your box? How?

3. In what ways has God's plan been different from your own?

time in prayer . . .

Thank God for his perfect plan and for his surprises. Ask him to help you better understand his ways and to help your ways become like his. Ask him to continue to reveal himself and his ways so you can get to know him better.

Who is this Jesus?

■ "But what about you?" he asked. "Who do you say that I am?" Simon Peter answered, "You are the Christ, the Son of the living God."

Matthew 16:15–16

what's in a name?

> God exalted him to the highest place and gave him the name that is above every name, that at the name of Jesus every knee should bow, in heaven and on earth and under the earth, and every tongue confess that Jesus Christ is Lord, to the glory of God the Father. (Philippians 2:9–11)

Jesus. Some thought he was crazy—a lunatic. Others believed him to be a great teacher, possibly a prophet. The Bible says he was the King of kings, yet he was born in a manger—not exactly where one would expect to find royalty. Some thought he would be a great warrior, but God's Word calls him the Prince of Peace. Jesus, himself, asked

Peter, "Who do you say I am?" Peter's answer? "You are the Christ, the Son of the living God" (Matthew 16:15–16).

What if we were posed that same question: Who is Jesus? What if Jesus asked us, "Who do you say I am?" How would I respond? How would you?

Jesus Christ. King of kings. Lord of lords. Holy One. The Bible has many names for the Son of God. But what does it *mean* to call him Savior? What does it mean to call him Lord? Is he really Lord of all in our lives?

I thought I would list some of the names of Jesus. I need to think about what they mean. As you read along, I encourage you to ponder them as well. Let God meet you where you are. Here goes . . .

- *Almighty*—all-knowing, all-powerful (Revelation 1:8)

- *Bread of Life*—giver of life, one who satis fies (John 6:35)

- *Creator*—architect of the universe, author of life (Colossians 1:16)

- *Counselor*—teacher, mentor, guide (Isaiah 9:6)

- *Deliverer*—one who rescues us from the bondage of sin (Romans 11:26)

- *Everlasting Father*—father who never leaves (Isaiah 9:6)

- *First and Last*—the beginning and the end (Revelation 1:17)

- *Good Shepherd*—shepherd who lays down his life for his sheep (John 10:11)

- *Holy One*—he who lived a sinless life (Acts 3:14)

- *I Am*—the eternal one (John 8:58)

- *Jesus of Nazareth*—a man who lived here and made his home among us (Matthew 21:11)

- *King of Kings*—ruler of all (1 Timothy 6:15)

- *Lamb of God*—sacrifice for our sins (John 1:29)

- *Light of the World*—a light to follow in the darkness (John 8:12)

- *Lord of All*—Lord of everything in heaven and on earth (Acts 10:36)

- *Mighty God*—the God of strength and power (Isaiah 9:6)

- *Prince of Peace*—peace in a disordered world (Isaiah 9:6)

- *Redeemer*—one who bought us back from Satan (Job 19:25)

- *Rock*—solid foundation, the cornerstone (1 Corinthians 10:4)

- *Resurrection and Life*—source of life after death (John 11:25)

- *Savior*—our Savior from sin (Luke 2:11)

- *Son of God*—God's beloved Son, his deity (Matthew 3:17)

- *Son of Man*—son of Mary and Joseph, human (Matthew 8:20)

- *Truth*—perfect truth in a world full of lies (John 14:6)

- *Word of God*—the living example of God's Word (John 1:1)

Wow. That's quite a list, and there are many more names. If we want to follow Jesus, we must get to know him. We must learn who he was, is, and claims to be. We need to know what his life was like, what words he used, and what choices he made. We need to get to know Jesus. Knowing his names is just the beginning—there is so much more. But the question he asked Peter is a good place to start, "Who do you say I am?"

questions to ponder . . .

1. Who is Jesus to you?

2. Which of the names is most meaningful to you? Why?

3. How can you get to know him better?

time in prayer . . .

Thank God for sending his Son and for the opportunity to have a relationship with him. Ask God to help you follow where he leads—wherever it takes you.

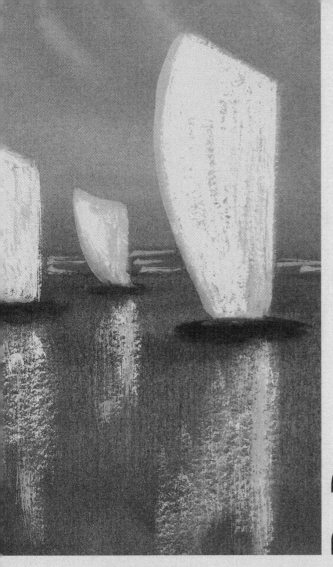

2

drop everything

drop everything

the nets are in the water
and hunger in their hearts
as they begin another ordinary day
they see You in the distance
standing on the shore
and no one is exactly sure what You'll say
but when You call
they don't hesitate at all and with

(Chorus)
no time to lose
they drop everything and follow You
don't care where to
they drop everything and follow You

i wonder what it'd be like
not to need a reason why
or want a little time
to think it all through
just to go
when You call me I would go with

(Chorus 2)
no time to lose
i'll drop everything and follow You
don't care where to
i'll drop everything and follow You

all You're asking for is all of me
help me leave the rest behind
leave it all behind
i wanna go with

(Chorus 2)

Scott Krippayne and Tony Miracle
© 1997 BMG Songs, Inc. (ASCAP), Above The Rim Music (ASCAP) and Meadowgreen Music/
Sugar Peter Songs (ASCAP). All rights on behalf of Above The Rim Music administered by
BMG Songs, Inc. (ASCAP)

26

"Drop Everything" began as a studio song. Tony Miracle and I were messing around one afternoon in the studio, trying to come up with musical ideas we liked, when we stumbled onto this one. It was a combination of him on the guitar and me on the piano. We went back and forth, changing each others chords, until we found the finished piece.

The lyric was one of the hardest ones I've ever written. I listened to the music over and over trying to find the right idea. I probably have eight or nine pages of lyrics that didn't seem to work. One day, out on the road, while I was having my quiet time on the bus, I read the passage in the Bible where Jesus called the first disciples. I was amazed at the way they followed him *immediately*. I tried to put myself in their shoes and understand what it was like. Later that evening I started to form the lyric in my head, and a few days later had it completed.

The first chorus speaks of the disciples' response, but the last ones talk of the response I hope to have. Each time I come across that passage in Scripture, and every time I sing this song, I'm amazed at how quickly the disciples abandoned everything to follow Jesus. I hope to do the same.

When Jesus
calls me,
will I go?

■ So they pulled their boats up on shore, left
everything and followed him.

Luke 5:11

how do i respond?

It continues to amaze me—Jesus called, and they followed. The New International Version uses words like "immediately" and "at once." The disciples didn't hesitate. Peter didn't say, "You know, I'd like to go, but my schedule's a little tight right now. Can we get together next week?" And Andrew didn't ask, "Where exactly are we going? And how long will we be gone?" James and John left their boat and their father to follow him. Jesus called, and they followed.

> As Jesus was walking beside the Sea of Galilee, he saw two brothers, Simon called Peter and his brother Andrew. They were casting a net

into the lake, for they were fishermen. "Come, follow me," Jesus said, "and I will make you fishers of men." At once they left their nets and followed him.

Going on from there, he saw two other brothers, James son of Zebedee and his brother John. They were in a boat with their father Zebedee, preparing their nets. Jesus called them, and immediately they left the boat and their father and followed him. (Matthew 4:18–22)

What was it about him that compelled the disciples to follow? Was it something he said? Was it the way he said it? How did they know *he* was the one to follow?

I find myself asking those questions. But the more important questions seem to be, When he calls me, will I go? and, How quickly will I respond? Usually, I wait too long. First, I wonder if it's really Jesus who's calling. Then, I look at my life—how busy things are and how comfortable I am—and I remember what an inconvenience change is. If I make it beyond that, I may try to reason with God.

But our Lord doesn't look for reasons, he looks for obedience. Obedience in the little things as well as the big. If I sense God calling me to spend more time with him, how long will I put it off? When our Lord calls, we need to follow. I, for one, am not very good at this. I don't act; I ask questions. "Why? Where? How long? Can I have some time to think about it?"

The disciples followed immediately. They didn't make excuses. Their beliefs resulted in taking action. They went—simply because it was Jesus who called.

The question remains: When Jesus calls us in the midst of our busy lives and hectic schedules, how will we respond? Will we hesitate and weigh our options, or will we do as the disciples did and follow the Way, the Truth, and the Life—Jesus Christ?

questions to ponder . . .

1. When your faith requires you to take action, how quickly do you respond?

2. What things in your life might keep you from following Jesus when he calls? People? Plans? Schedule?

3. What can you do to prepare yourself to go when he calls?

time in prayer . . .

Thank God for the disciples' example of following quickly when they were called. Ask God for ears to hear his voice. Ask him to help prepare you to be ready and willing to go when he calls. And ask him to deal with the things in your life that might keep you from following him.

everything

drop everything

What will I have to leave behind if I follow Jesus?

Then he said to them all: "If anyone would come after me, he must deny himself and take up his cross daily and follow me."

Luke 9:23

the cost

Jesus probably didn't have much more than the clothes on his back . . . I've got a closet full.

Jesus traveled frequently—on foot, along dusty roads, for miles and miles . . . I prefer the comforts of home and a nice warm bed.

Jesus didn't have many possessions to detract him from his work . . . I enjoy listening to music in my car on my way home to watch Sportscenter.

Jesus lived a simple life . . . sometimes my life seems so complicated.

What does it mean to follow Jesus? I believe it means, in essence, the willingness to *drop everything.* It may mean leaving the comforts of my home and following his call to a distant land; it may mean choosing to go back home to learn to love and forgive someone who hurt me years ago.

Dropping everything for his sake will mean different things to different people, but it always means choosing him over all else, and it means that once I've made that choice, I don't look back.

Do you remember the Luke 9 conversation Jesus had with three men as he traveled the road to Jerusalem and to his impending death?

> As they were walking along the road, a man said to him, "I will follow you wherever you go."
>
> Jesus replied, "Foxes have holes and birds of the air have nests, but the Son of Man has no place to lay his head." (vv. 57–58)

This first man made a big promise—"I will follow you wherever you go"—and Jesus challenged his promise. "Do you really know what you're getting into? Can you back up that promise with action?" Jesus was asking.

> [Jesus] said to another man, "Follow me."
>
> But the man replied, "Lord, first let me go and bury my father."
>
> Jesus said to him, "Let the dead bury their own dead, but you go and proclaim the kingdom of God." (vv. 59–60)

Does this seem harsh to you? Scholars tell us that this man's father was probably not even dead yet. This guy was looking for an excuse to put off following Jesus until a more convenient time—perhaps after his father died.

Don't we sometimes do the same thing? "Uh, yeah, I want to follow Jesus—but not now. I'm still young. I want to have some fun first. There's plenty of time for Jesus later." Or, "Sure, I want to follow Jesus. Just let me get my career on track; then I'll make time for him in my life."

But Jesus demands first place in our lives, and he insists that we follow him *now*. William Barclay, in his commentary on the gospel of Luke, says that in everything important there is a crucial moment; if we don't respond when we first feel the stirrings in our hearts, we may never respond. While the grace of God is everlasting, and while his arms are always open to us, for some of us, if we don't do it now, we never will. If we ignore the call of Jesus today, we may not hear it tomorrow.

> Still another said, "I will follow you, Lord; but first let me go back and say good-by to my family."
> Jesus replied, "No one who puts his hand to the plow and looks back is fit for service in the kingdom of God." (vv. 61–62)

Following Jesus means dropping everything, turning our faces toward him, and never looking back. Some people may look like they're following Jesus on the outside, but their hearts are forever looking back at what they've given up, where they could have gone, who they could have been.

Obviously, I have some work to do. What about you? If Jesus were hanging out in your hometown today, would you follow him? Would you follow him *wherever* he led you? Would you follow him *now*? Would you *drop everything*? The answers might not make us feel all that comfortable, but Jesus didn't come for our comfort. He came so that we might know him, so that we might follow him.

Following Christ will not always be easy. Christ's path eventually led to a cross. Following him will bring risks; it will bring persecution. Some people will call you crazy, others may even try to hurt you. There are still countries where it's illegal to proclaim the Gospel of Jesus Christ.

And the sacrifice will be great. We will be asked to surrender all we have and are to Jesus Christ, allowing him to be Lord of everything in our lives. We must lay down our agenda for the sake of his. He calls us to deny ourselves, pick up his cross, and follow him daily.

There are many things in my own life that I continually need to surrender so that I will be free to follow Jesus. My dreams, desires, plans, and possessions—all these can hinder me from following where he leads. I need to continually lay down these things—everything—daily, for the sake of following Christ. The disciples dropped everything and followed him. Will I? Will you?

questions to ponder . . .

1. What comforts would you have a hard time leaving behind for Jesus?

2. Which of the three men Jesus talked with on the road are you most like? The one who made a promise to follow without knowing what was involved; the one who wanted to put off following later; or the one who kept looking back to what he was leaving?

3. What is Jesus asking you to let go of?

4. What would it look like in your life to take up the cross and follow Jesus daily?

time in prayer . . .

Thank God for sending his Son for us to follow. Ask God to help take away any hindrances that keep you from following him. Ask him to bring to mind the areas in your life where you could follow closer. Ask him to help you to pick up your cross and follow him daily.

3

all my days

all my days

in prodigal days
You didn't release me
You sent angels to keep me
You guided me home

in desperate days
i could see no tomorrow
You entered my sorrow
You cradled me close

all my days i've been so foolish
all my days i've run so far
but all my days You've been so faithful
You never left me in all my days

in prosperous days
when i trusted good fortune
and my heart became hardened
You shattered my pride

in humbling days
when i begged for forgiveness
it was already given
You had given Your life

blinded by the moment
reeling with emotion
i never saw Your hands around me
caring for my soul
the work of love and wisdom
is too large for human vision
but grace has followed
everywhere i go

Scott Krippayne and Douglas Kaine McKelvey
© 1995 BMG Songs, Inc. (ASCAP), Above The Rim Music (ASCAP) and Ariose Music
(ASCAP). All rights on behalf of Above The Rim Music administerd by BMG Songs, Inc.
(ASCAP)

■ THE STORY BEHIND THE SONG

Doug and I met for the first time at a Chinese restaurant. We sat at a back table, ate lunch, and talked about songs. I was writing for my first record, and I was looking for a song that addressed God's faithfulness—even when we're not so faithful. Doug reached into a folder and pulled out the lyric for "All My Days."

I was dumbfounded. Did someone call and tell this guy my life story? The words blew me away. Doug had captured just what I wanted to say. We talked awhile about the possibilities, until, eventually, I had to get back to work. I was delivering airline tickets for a travel agency at the time, and I had a full afternoon. But I really wanted to work on the song, so I placed the lyric on the passenger seat of my little Honda. (Don't try this at home—it can cause severe car wrecks.)

But fortunately, that afternoon there was no wreck, just music. I worked, I sang, I drove, and I wrote. By the time I got home, I had a pretty good idea of what the music would sound like. I kept the lyric with me for a few days and continued to tweak the music. My wife, Katy, and I listened to it together, bobbing our heads and humming along. The final result is still one of my favorite songs. The music is a blast to play and sing, and the message is one I will always need to hear.

When I am foolish, will God still be faithful?

■ Your love, O Lord, reaches to the heavens, your faithfulness to the skies.

Psalm 36:5

my foolishness, his faithfulness

> I will sing of the Lord's great love forever; with
> my mouth I will make your faithfulness known
> through all generations. I will declare that your
> love stands firm forever, that you established
> your faithfulness in heaven itself. (Psalm 89:1–2)

I feel a lot like the psalmist. I want to talk about, sing
about, and share God's faithfulness. I've experienced it
firsthand.

One year after I accepted Jesus as my Lord and Savior,
it was time to head off to college. I grew up in a rather
small town, in a somewhat protective family, and I was a
bit naive about the big city and a big college. My new

experiences were eye-opening to say the least. I felt lost among 35,000 other students. I was Student Number 8832091—I felt more known by my number than my name.

During my first quarter there, I could go to classes for a week and not see anyone I knew on campus. I was lonely and wanted desperately to fit in. Having those feelings and living away from my parents for the first time made me quite susceptible to peer pressure. And it didn't take that much pressure for me to cave in: "Do you want a beer?" was usually enough to do it. Without going into all the details, my Bible went on the shelf, and I went to the parties.

I made a lot of bad choices my freshman year, but the Lord refused to let me go. I wanted to put our relationship on hold, but he wasn't willing to let that happen. God pursued me and he was persistent. And I'm glad he was. I knew the choices I was making weren't the best and that God had something better, but I continued to disobey. I knew my lifestyle wasn't his will, but I was selfish. I'd look at my Bible, think of my relationship with the Lord, and find it hard to face him—a holy God.

But through it all, he never gave up on me. He used different people in my life to remind me of the truth. He would bring people into my room, and they would ask about my Bible. I started getting invited to a college fellowship that met near campus. It soon became evident that I would have to address my relationship with the Lord. I would have to face God. Eventually, I began going to that college fellowship. I started reading my Bible again, I confessed my sins, and I began to make better choices.

I was foolish, but the Lord was faithful. I may have let him down, but he wasn't going to let me go. When I ran away, he guided me back home. I broke my promise to live for him, but he kept his promise—he didn't leave. He loved me through my struggles.

Sometimes I look back and wish I could live that year over and make some different choices—not be so foolish. But I learned a great deal about the character of God during that time. I learned that he loves us enough to pursue a relationship with us. And I learned that he is persistent in his pursuit. No one is a lost cause. We have a God who is faithful and a God who forgives.

Think of some examples of God's faithfulness in your own life. Has he brought you through some difficult times? Are you in the midst of a hardship now? Do you see the Lord's hand in your life? Keep watching. Our Lord will prove himself faithful. He has proven himself so time and time again.

As we see the Lord demonstrate his character—his love and his faithfulness in our lives—I'm amazed. And I'm grateful. And I want to leave my foolishness behind and become like the psalmist and "sing of the Lord's great love forever" and make his "faithfulness known through all generations." Let's go out and make it known.

questions to ponder . . .

1. What foolishness have you pursued in your life?

2. How has the Lord responded?

3. How has he demonstrated his faithfulness in your life?

4. With whom can you share what he's done?

time in prayer . . .

Thank God for his faithfulness. Thank him for the ways he demonstrates it. Thank him for pursuing a relationship with you. Ask him to help you be faithful to him.

How can I know

God is working

in my life?

> So we fix our eyes not on what is seen, but on what is unseen. For what is seen is temporary, but what is unseen is eternal.
>
> 2 Corinthians 4:18

fingerprints

Every once in a while we catch a glimpse of God at work—and when we do, it's an awesome realization. Sometimes the veil is pulled back for a split second, and we see a tiny piece of eternity. Perhaps we're allowed to witness someone accepting Jesus as Lord and Savior, or maybe we realize that a handful of coincidences may not really be "coincidental" at all. We do, on occasion, get a peek of our Lord at work, but most of the time we don't see it. Sometimes we're too busy to notice, and sometimes we're looking the wrong way. Or maybe—even if we knew the exact time and place to look—maybe sometimes his wondrous workings are beyond our ability to see.

Sometimes I look at my life and wonder if I am really growing in Christ, if I'm really becoming the man God wants me to be. Much of the time, I just can't see much change. But as I look back over the years, I have a better view of how he's worked. I see times when he relentlessly pursued me even when I was not pursuing him; I see his efforts to teach me to be less selfish; I see little gifts of encouragement when I felt alone. I see fingerprints of his love.

Our Lord finishes what he starts. Paul is confident of this as he speaks to the Philippians, "He who began a good work in you will carry it on to completion until the day of Christ Jesus" (Philippians 1:6). God has begun a good work in each of us, and he will bring it to completion.

So even when I can't see him, I want to trust that the Lord is working. He was working when I began attending YoungLife and later began a personal relationship with Jesus. He was working my freshman year in college as he used my foolishness to teach me about his faithfulness. He has walked me through tough decisions and carried me through difficult times. I don't always see him; at times I wonder if he's there at all, but time and time again I see his fingerprints—fingerprints of hope, fingerprints of mercy, fingerprints of grace.

What's God doing in your life now? Does he seem near, far away, or somewhere in between? What is he teaching you? Look back over the last few years of your life and look for God's fingerprints. Do you see some areas in your life—and your heart—that now bear his fingerprints?

We have a mysterious God, and he is sometimes hard to understand. He is so awesome, we cannot begin to comprehend all that he is or how he works. His ways are different from ours; he looks at life differently than we do. He looks at people differently too.

I wonder what he sees in me. I wonder how he'll work in my life in the next year. I wonder what he's doing right now.

questions to ponder . . .

1. Have you ever caught a glimpse of God at work? What was he doing?

2. What work has God started in you? Envision how your life will be when he finishes.

3. Looking back, what are some ways he has worked in your life? What fingerprints has he left in your life?

4. What may hinder you from seeing even more of him?

time in prayer . . .

Thank God for the work he's doing—the work you see and the work you don't see. Thank him for beginning a work in you that he will one day bring to completion. Thank him for the times he's carried you. Ask him for eyes to see him at work so that you may join him where he's working.

4

from the heart

from the heart

this world is so full of demands
all kinds of ways to busy my hands
i get comfortable with the routine
and don't stop to wonder what matters to me
maybe it's time to clean my house
and make room for the things that i care about

(Chorus)
let me say what i mean
and believe what i say
let my life come from the heart
let my actions come out of the prayers that i pray
let my life come from the heart

i'm wasting way too much time
passing the days as my life passes by
phoning it in, playing it safe
taking for granted the gifts that You gave
i want to live in the here and now
with the passion to make every single day count

(Chorus)

Lord, let my heart be set on You
in all that i am and all i do

Scott Krippayne and Steve Siler
© 1997 BMG Songs, Inc. (ASCAP), Above The Rim Music (ASCAP) and Magnolia Hill Music
(ASCAP) (A Division of McSpadden-Smith Music). All rights on behalf of Above The Rim
Music administered by BMG Songs, Inc. (ASCAP)

■ THE STORY BEHIND THE SONG

When Steve and I sat down to write this song, the lyric came relatively quickly. We were both passionate about the idea. Of course . . . the song talks about living life with passion. In the bridge, we wanted to make sure the lyric touched on the state of the heart. Living a life of sincerity is great, but ultimately our hearts need to be set on the Lord—focused on him and his will for our lives.

The music didn't fall into place quite as easily and took a bit more time. We fumbled around with various melodies but eventually discovered some music we both loved—music that we thought captured the urgency and passion of living a life from the heart.

from the heart

Who is Jesus to me?

> ■ We have seen and testify that the Father has sent his Son to be the Savior of the world.
>
> 1 John 4:14

sorting things out

One very busy afternoon, I received a rather interesting phone call. A church where I was scheduled to do a concert wanted a statement of faith from me. Apparently, they wanted to know a little more about the artists who would play for their church.

But my wife, Katy, and I were in the middle of packing to move. Our apartment looked like a war zone. Boxes were stacked to the ceiling, we couldn't find anything we needed, and to top it all off, I was heading out on a tour in a couple of weeks.

The church's request was a valid one. It's my response that bothers me. Instead of taking a few minutes to jot down a paragraph about what I believe, I obtained a copy of the Apostle's Creed, signed it, sent it off, and got back to packing.

But now that I've had some time to think, I'm really troubled. That "stuff" I was too busy for was my beliefs—the beliefs that supposedly affect how I live and how I respond to simple requests. But they didn't affect me that day. I was "too busy." There were dishes to pack, phone numbers to change, and mail to be forwarded. It's not that these things were bad—they needed to be done. But I had allowed them to take over my life. I had let the stress of the move take charge of my priorities. I had let my circumstances control my life.

It had been awhile since I had thought about God. It had been even longer since I had slowed down and stopped to spend some unhurried time with him. It was time for a change. It was time to ask some serious questions. It was time to pay a little less attention to the clutter in the apartment and a little more attention to the clutter in my life.

What do I believe? I believe in God. I believe he sent his Son to die for my sins.

What do I value? I value honesty and integrity. I value a personal relationship with Jesus Christ.

Who is Jesus to me? He is my Savior. And he is the Lord of my life.

Does what I believe impact the way I live? Not always. I can make a list of what I believe and what I value; but, sadly, that doesn't always result in action. At times my life reveals that I value myself over others and my desires over God's will. When I look closely at my life, I see that some changes are needed. I need to do more than sort out my closet; I must sort out my priorities and figure out what really matters.

I want to have a passion for life. I want the life I live to mean something. Each time I read Paul's charge to the Colossians, I'm moved by it. "Whatever you do, work at it with all your heart, as working for the Lord, not for men, since you know that you will receive an inheritance from the Lord as a reward. It is the Lord Christ you are serving" (Colossians 3:23–24). I want to live like that—in the little things, in the big—in all I do! Paul speaks of "sincerity of heart" and "reverence for the Lord" (v. 22)—I want these things in my life.

God works in funny ways. He took a song I wrote more than a year earlier and used it to shine a light on my life concerning my response to that church. I want to let the Lord of my life be the Lord of my life. I want him to be the priority. I want to spend more time in the Word of God, learning about him and his ways. I want to know what I believe and be ready to respond the next time I get the call for a statement of faith.

Here's a little challenge: Take a good look at your own life. Ask yourself some tough questions. Do you need to do any "housecleaning?" Do you need to make any changes? Let's pursue a deeper, more intimate walk with a living God—together.

questions to ponder . . .

1. What are your priorities? Do you need to make any changes? If so, what?

2. What do you believe? What do you value?

3. Do your beliefs affect the way you live? How?

4. What changes do you need to make in your life so that your life more accurately reflects your beliefs?

time in prayer . . .

Thank God for never being too busy for you. Thank him for always having time and listening well. Ask him to set your priorities his way. Give him permission to make changes in your life—to do some housecleaning. Thank him that his way is the best way.

from the heart

Is life passing me by while I'm wasting time?

■ Teach us to number our days aright, that we may gain a heart of wisdom.

Psalm 90:12

every second counts

We finally entered the nineties. A few months ago, Katy and I purchased our first computer. I was so excited. I figured it would help me get more things done in more efficient ways. I would have easy access to figures and phone numbers, and I could do research while I explored the net. The world was at my fingertips. And that was my problem.

The novelty of having a computer was staggering. I was completely intrigued. I logged long hours learning my way around, playing games, and e-mailing friends. I spent so much time on the computer that I wasn't getting anything else done. My songwriting slowed, I seldom went outside, and communication with Katy was deteriorating rapidly. I had found such an engrossing way to pass the time that I wasn't living life anymore.

One morning, I woke up and headed down the hall toward the computer. As I sat down, I noticed a small piece of paper attached to the monitor. It read, "Be very careful, then, how you live—not as unwise but as wise, making the most of every opportunity, because the days are evil" (Ephesians 5:15–16). Katy had definitely noticed my long hours and late nights in front of the screen, and she was lovingly nudging me with the truth. Using God's Word, she reminded me that each moment is precious and worth living and that I needed to make wise choices as to how I use the time each day.

Looking at that scripture from Ephesians, I realized I was not being careful, and I was not really living. I was being careless with my time, and opportunities were passing me by on my left and right—a chance to take a walk in the park or go for a run, a chance to call an old friend or write a letter to my dad. There were opportunities to live, think, and experience all around me, and I was stuck staring at a small television screen.

Please don't get me wrong; I'm not against computers. They can be useful, helpful, and time-saving machines. What concerns me is wasting time. And I can waste time doing almost anything—the computer was just my most recent accomplice.

I want to live. I want to make the most of the time God has given. The days are short, and our lives here are limited. God has created an amazing planet, and there is much to experience. Take a minute right now to look outside. What do you see? Take a good look at what God has created. What's the weather like? Think about your family for a moment—and your friends. Who haven't you talked to in a while? Put down this book and give that person a call. Write someone a letter. (Or e-mail them, if you wish.)

God has given us family and friends—people who love us and people to love. And over time we will develop new relationships that we haven't even dreamed of yet.

Jesus came so we might find true life. "The thief comes only to steal and kill and destroy; I have come that they may have life and have it to the full" (John 10:10). I don't want to waste time just getting through another day. I don't want life to pass me by while I'm staring at a television or surfing the net. I want to live my life for Jesus and live it to the fullest. Each moment is precious, and I never want to lose sight of that. Jesus came to give us life. Let's not take that life for granted; let's live it!

questions to ponder . . .

1. Do you ever waste time? What is your preferred method?

2. What's the difference between really living and just passing time?

3. What changes can you make to waste less time and live more?

time in prayer . . .

Thank God for the gift of today. Thank him for every hour, minute, and second. Ask him how to best use the time you've been given. Ask God to show you what it means to live life to the fullest. Ask him for his help in doing so.

5

His

His

lately i've been thinking 'bout myself
thinking i don't need nobody else
so sure that i had all the answers
i lost sight of all that really matters—that it's . . .

(Chorus)
His grace that saved me
His death that gave me life
His wounds that healed me
with a loving sacrifice
'cause i'm His

if you see some good thing that i've done
it's simply a reflection of the Son
it's His will that i'm reaching for
'cause my life is not my own anymore—no 'cause it's . . .

(Chorus 2)
His grace that saved me
His death that gave me life
His wounds that healed me
with a loving sacrifice
His blood that bought me
my sin that He forgives
His voice that calls me
let me live the life i live
'cause i'm His

i'll lay down my pride
and the gifts i've been given
'cause i am a child
of the Father in heaven

Scott Krippayne and Steve Siler
© 1997 BMG Songs, Inc. (ASCAP), Above The Rim Music (ASCAP) and Magnolia Hill Music
(ASCAP) (A Division of McSpadden-Smith Music). All rights on behalf of Above The Rim Music
administered by BMG Songs, Inc. (ASCAP)

You've probably heard about people who sing in the shower—maybe you're one of them. I sure am. I've been known to take twenty- or thirty-minute showers just because I'm into a song. It was on one such morning that the idea for "His" began to develop.

The title was one I'd had for a while; I just couldn't get anywhere with it. I wanted to write a song about perspective—taking the focus off of myself and placing it back on the Lord where it belongs. I was just about ready to rinse the shampoo from my hair when the chorus started to take shape. I continued to pursue the idea until all the hot water was gone. I then had to move on to more traditional songwriting methods.

Steve Siler and I got together a couple of days later and sat down with a guitar and a notepad. He caught on to the idea quickly, and it was a rather painless afternoon. After a few hours of writing, we had finished a song.

So if you're one of those people who sing in the shower, keep it up. You never know what may happen—or what God may teach you.

How many more layers of selfishness will I discover in myself?

■ Do nothing out of selfish ambition or vain conceit, but in humility consider others better than yourselves. Each of you should look not only to your own interests, but also to the interests of others.

Philippians 2:3–4

all about me

I am so selfish sometimes. I can be so intent on getting my needs met that I don't even see the needs of those around me. I become so consumed with my selfish ambitions that I forget what really matters. Sometimes I think what I have to say is so important that I won't listen to what anyone else is saying. I think *my* way is the right way, and things will get done when I can fit them into *my* schedule.

My.

Me.

Mine.

God has invested some time in trying to increase my awareness of my selfishness. Sometimes he's taught me through sermons, other times through songs. As I began to see more and more areas in my life where I needed work, I thought to myself, "How much more could there be?"

When I got married, a whole new layer of selfishness was uncovered. After twenty-some-odd years of meeting just my needs, my focus changed dramatically. Now there were two of us—in close quarters. I loved Katy and wanted to serve her. I wanted her needs to be met. But it was a struggle sometimes. I was used to having things my way. The Lord began to show me that *more* changes needed to take place. I needed to think of my wife first, before myself. We are now three years into our marriage, and I've grown some . . . but I have a long way to go.

The reason I'm so concerned with my selfishness is that if it's not causing me to sin now, it can quickly lead to it. I may choose my way over God's way. I may pursue my desires instead of God's plan. When I'm intent on serving myself, I can't serve God. When I'm following my own will—set on having my own way—I push God out of the way. And the point of having a Savior is admitting that I can't save myself, that I can't do it on my own—and yet my actions prove that I think otherwise. I continue to pursue my own needs when what I really need is God.

How can I be less self-centered? As with most things, the move from selfishness to caring more about others and their needs seems to be a process. I long for God to reach in and remove every ounce of selfishness from my heart, but the process is a lengthy one. He tends to reveal one area of selfishness at a time. My prayer is that I will let him have his way with me.

I'm trying to continually place my trust in God. I'm trying to allow God to change me. I'm trying to focus my attention on others and take it off myself. I'm striving to listen more and talk less. I'm attempting to pray more for others. I'm looking for ways to serve rather than be served. The process is not easy, and I miss the mark quite a bit. I still want my own way sometimes, but deep down I know that God's way is best. I long for my will to be conformed to his.

I'm still selfish, but I'm confident that God is changing me from the inside out and will one day bring that work to completion.

questions to ponder . . .

1. Have you ever been selfish? How have you been selfish with your time, your money, your possessions, or in pursuit of your ambitions?

2. How can you become more other-centered?

3. What are some practical ways you can serve those around you?

4. Who can you pray for? What friends? What enemies?

time in prayer . . .

Thank God for loving you as you are—in spite of your selfishness. Ask him to deal with any selfishness you may have. Ask him to help you consider others better than yourself. Ask God to show you the needs of those around you and how you might help.

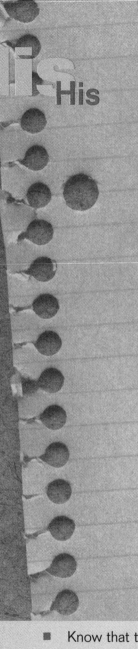

His

How can I make time for the creator of time?

- Know that the Lord is God. It is he who made us, and we are his; we are his people, the sheep of his pasture.

  Psalm 100:3

a grain of sand

It was a lazy September evening, and I had just finished a concert in Florida. When I returned to the hotel, I called my wife and got ready for bed. It was about midnight when I hung up the phone, but I was still wide awake. I decided to take a walk along the beach.

Life had been pretty crazy lately, and I hadn't spent much time with God. "I'll get to it later" was my usual justification. But "later" always came and went. It seemed I couldn't *make* time for the *Creator* of time.

As I walked along the shore, I thought about all the things going on in my life. There were so many thoughts running through my head, I couldn't even think straight. I needed to slow down. I needed to get my mind on something else. I stared at the ocean and listened to the sound of the waves. I wiggled my toes in the sand, and slowly my perspective began to change.

I looked up and down the coastline as far as I could see; God had created it all. I looked down at my feet and started to feel about as small as one of those grains of sand. God was so big and so in control, and yet he had time for me.

In a matter of moments, I had gone from a mess to amazed. I was amazed that God loved me, amazed that he sent his Son to die for me, amazed that he forgives my sin, amazed that he knows my name and calls me his child.

I'm his.

It's not about me; it's about him.

It's his grace that saved me. There's nothing I can do—I can't do enough good deeds, say enough prayers, or spend enough Sundays at church; nothing I do can make me holy. I am a sinner. But the grace of God, through his Son, Jesus Christ, saves me from my sin.

It's his death that gives me life. Jesus' death on a cross offers me life—eternal life—with God himself.

It's his blood that bought me. Someone had to pay for my sins. Someone had to suffer the consequences. Jesus was the only one qualified to pay the price, and he did so willingly; he died for my sin.

It's his voice that calls me. God calls me to follow him. Because of what Jesus did on the Cross, I'm offered a relationship with God. And when he calls, I want to follow.

When we struggle for control in our lives, the remedy is simple. We must take the focus off ourselves and place it back on God. When we consider who he is and what he's done, our perspective straightens out quickly.

A wave washed over my feet. I was caught up with God's creation, his majesty, and his sacrifice.

> I have been crucified with Christ and I no longer live, but Christ lives in me. The life I live in the body, I live by faith in the Son of God, who loved me and gave himself for me. (Galatians 2:20)

I have been bought at a price; my life is not my own. And when I think about the one who paid that price and the one who created the universe, there's not a lot of room left for my selfishness.

questions to ponder . . .

1. How does your life sometimes get out of control? Where do you turn when your life gets crazy?

2. What is it about being out in nature that helps us see things in a better perspective?

3. What about God amazes you?

4. How can being filled with God dispel selfishness?

time in prayer . . .

Thank God for who he is and what he's done. Thank him for being in control. Thank him for his perfect perspective on life and ask him to show that perspective to you. Thank him for the ways he amazes you and reminds you that he is God.

How does true humility act?

- He has showed you, O man, what is good. And what does the Lord require of you? To act justly and to love mercy and to walk humbly with your God.

Micah 6:8

how proud am i?

Humility has always puzzled me. I've always understood humility to be a good thing, but what it should look like in my life was a bit confusing. I used to think that it meant belittling myself. If someone gave me a compliment or said, "Good job," I would flat out contradict them: "No, I'm not that good," I'd say with my head down. "I'm really nobody."

I knew I was supposed to be humble, so I tried to *act* humble. But that's what it was—an act. I acted a certain way because I thought it was expected of me. It was simply a game—false humility. I wasn't really humble at all.

So what is true humility? Humility is considering others better than yourself (Philippians 2:3). Getting to know God and understanding my need for him humbles me. When I realize that it's his grace that saves me—and not anything I do—it becomes harder to be proud.

Why would we want to be humble? Humility was part of Jesus' character to the extent that he became like a servant. If we want to follow Jesus, we must emulate his humility.

> Your attitude should be the same as that of Christ Jesus: who, being in very nature God, did not consider equality with God something to be grasped, but made himself nothing, taking the very nature of a servant. . . . He humbled himself and became obedient to death—even death on a cross! (Philippians 2:5–8)

Jesus spent his life caring for others—not himself—even to the point of death. Why should we be humble? Because Jesus is.

What does humility look like? Humility doesn't look like self-degredation. It isn't deflecting compliments. Humble people acknowledge the gifts God has given them as just that—gifts. They don't think of themselves as better than others—or worse. In his book *Mere Christianity,* C. S. Lewis gives my favorite defintion of a humble individual.

> Probably all you will think about him is that he seemed a cheerful, intelligent chap who took a real interest in what you said to *him.* . . . He will not be thinking about humility: he will not be thinking about himself at all.

Sounds like an attractive quality to me.

So, if humility is the goal, *how do we achieve it?* We must first admit that we are proud—proud in the sense that we think of ourselves as better than others. If we can't admit our pride, we may become proud of our "humility." Humility doesn't necessarily come from *trying* to be humble; it generally arises when we are caught up in serving, actively listening to, and genuinely caring about someone else's needs. Humility can become a way of life if we constantly think about others before ourselves.

So there it is—humility. It still puzzles me, but not quite as much as it used to. Honest humility is simply a grateful and unselfish outlook on life: loving others well and being thankful that God loves us.

questions to ponder . . .

1. What's the difference between self-degredation and true humility?

2. In what ways are you proud—thinking yourself better than others?

3. How do you view the gifts and talents God has given you?

4. How does understanding your need for God increase your humility?

5. Think of someone you consider humble. What is he or she like?

time in prayer . . .

Thank God for the example of humility he gave in his Son, Jesus. Ask him to show you what it means to be humble. Ask him to reveal any areas of unhealthy pride in your life and to help you become a more humble person.

6

way back home

way back home

had coffee in seattle
wrote a song in tennessee
i spent a week in houston
and I watched too much tv
i meet a lot of people
but still feel all alone, and . . .

(Chorus)
i want to find my way back home

i rode a bus through kansas
got a ticket in st. paul
played a show in carolina
where I had no voice at all
the reason why I started
seems so long ago . . . and

(Chorus)

i know there's something missing
and i know that i need to find my way back home
find my way back home

i dream about the day
when i will fall to my knees
at the feet of a Friend
'cause maybe there's a chance
that we could sing together again

(Chorus)

I had never written a song this way. Charlie, the record producer, thought it would be fun to try something new—something to open up the creative flow. All we had was a rough drum part and he asked me to sing—whatever—and we'd record it. No pressure. I believe his comment was, "Go play in the sandbox for a while." So I did. It took a few minutes to get past my inhibitions, but pretty soon I was singing "la-la's" and other nonsense lyrics to whatever melodies came to mind. After ten minutes, I was finished. Now it was co-writer Tony's turn. And then Charlie's. After everything was said and done, we had about thirty minutes of vocalizing on tape. As we listened back, we picked out our favorite parts, began to piece them together, and presto . . . music! Somewhere amid the nonsense lyrics, I used the phrase "my way back home" a few times—and it stuck.

After numerous rewrites and lots of coffee, I finally completed the lyric. I tried to describe some of my travels over the past couple of years, as well as capture my prodigal-son tendencies. I had been to quite a number of places; I had sung a lot of songs; but the Lord wasn't always at the center—and deep down I wanted and *needed* him to be. This song simply describes the progression of that time of my life: how I began to go my own way, the emptiness that accompanies self-willed living, and my journey back—finally falling at the feet of my heavenly Father.

way back home

How did I get here, and how do I get back to where I belong?

■ Have mercy on me, O God, according to your unfailing love; according to your great compassion blot out my transgressions. Wash away all my iniquity and cleanse me from my sin.

Psalm 51:1–2

what road am i on?

Have you ever felt like the prodigal son? Have you ever felt like running away? Maybe you wanted to do your own thing for a while—you know, get out and explore the world—so you packed your bags and left. Or maybe it was a bit more subtle. Perhaps you took a few steps away from your Father each day, pushing the limits little by little, until one day you woke up and realized how far away you were.

Have you been there—cold and confused, wondering how you got so far away from home?

Have you been there—tired and weary, comparing where you used to be to where you are now?

Have you been there—empty and alone, longing for your faith and a friend and trying to find your way back home?

I have.

I most certainly have been in that place.

And I found myself asking: How did I get here? And how do I get back to where I belong?

I've loved music since I was a little boy. I loved to listen to it, play it, and write it. Music moved me. I began taking songwriting seriously when I was in high school. It was an outlet, of sorts. There was something inside me—a feeling, a thought, an idea—looking for a way out. Singing and songwriting were the ways I expressed what was going on inside. When I met Jesus, I had a new relationship and new experiences to write about. It was a natural progression—God was changing my heart and my life and out came the songs. I didn't care about making money or whether a bunch of people liked my voice or the songs—I simply had to write. I'd sing for anyone who would listen.

A few years ago, I was given an opportunity to make a record. I was really excited. Not only would I be able to make a living doing something I loved, but more people would hear the songs—and hopefully relate to them.

Over time I became more and more consumed with the business side of what I was doing. Where was my song on the chart? How many records were being sold? It was a slow and subtle process. In concert, I'd find myself not thinking about the song I was singing—just simply going through the motions. God wanted to be the center of my life, and I was leaving him out of the process. I had forgotten why I was singing, why I was writing.

Finally one day I realized that something was wrong; something was missing. Every note, every song, and the ability to sing is a gift from God; but I had taken those gifts and gone my own direction. I wanted God to be the center again. I wanted to love what I was doing. I wanted to give the gifts back to the Giver. The only question was how? Luke 15 tells the story: "So he got up and went to his father."

The prodigal son headed for home, so I decided to do the same. I knelt down and prayed. I asked God for his forgiveness and his help. "But while he was still a long way off, his father saw him and was filled with compassion for him; he ran to his son, threw his arms around him and kissed him."

The father saw his son and ran to embrace him. Our heavenly Father does the same. If you feel like you've run too far away to come home—you're wrong. If you think you've been away too long to return—it's not too late. We all make mistakes. We may all try our own road once in a while, but we have a compassionate and gracious God. If we seek him, we will find him, and his love is unconditional. The way back may be rough and it may be long, but we have a Father who will run to meet us and guide us home.

questions to ponder . . .

1. Have you ever run from God? Or have you ever walked away slowly—step by step? Where are you now in your life's journey?

2. If you've ever left home, what lured you away? What did you learn from the experience?

3. Have you ever felt you were so far away from God's heart that you couldn't go home? What does the story of the prodigal son say about that?

4. How is your relationship with your heavenly Father right now?

time in prayer . . .

Thank God for his love for you. Thank him for his continual pursuit of you. Thank him that you can never run so far away that you can't return home. Ask God to be the center of your life. Ask him to guide and direct your path and to help you grow in your relationship with him.

way back home

Is it possible
that there's a
place for me in my
Father's home?

■ But our citizenship is in heaven. And we
eagerly await a Savior from there, the Lord
Jesus Christ.

Philippians 3:20

going home

I love flopping down on a familiar, comfortable bed after restless nights in hotel rooms. I relish that first bite of a home-cooked meal after a week of eating greasy fast food. And when Katy is expecting me to return, coming home is even more amazing. I can't imagine anything better than opening the front door and seeing the welcoming arms of my loving wife. I drop my baggage and fall into her wonderful embrace. There's nothing like it—coming home.

But for some of you, coming home may not be such a great experience. In today's world, abuse is painfully real. Physical, mental, and emotional abuse are all too prevalent. Coming home sometimes involves returning to difficult family situations or painful memories. I've met people who have wanted to get as far away from home as possible, hoping never to return. Unfortunately, not everyone experiences joyous homecomings.

But life is a continuing journey. The life you now live is not the end; it's the process. We are all headed somewhere. As children of God, we are like aliens and strangers in this world—this is not our home. What will it be like, one day, to come home to our heavenly Father—to see him face to face, to fall into the arms of the one who loves us more than we can comprehend? "He will wipe every tear from their eyes. There will be no more death or mourning or crying or pain, for the old order of things has passed away" (Revelation 21:4). For those of you who love coming home, my guess is that heaven will be even better. And for those of you who have difficult home lives, heaven will be far greater than anything you could ever dream.

No more pain.

No more crying.

No more death.

No more mourning.

Sounds pretty amazing, doesn't it? Just the description of heaven is comforting—imagine what the real thing will be. A home with God is something to look forward to, a hope to hold on to when things around us seem to be falling apart.

When the circumstances, pain, and struggles of this life are frustrating, we must remember that we're on a journey and that we're not yet home. Persevere, one day at a time, as you get to know the one who is greater than your circumstances. Remember the words of Paul, "But one thing I do: Forgetting what is behind and straining toward what is ahead, I press on toward the goal to win the prize for which God has called me heavenward in Christ Jesus" (Philippians 3:13–14).

One day the pain will be over. This journey will be complete. One day we will go home to our heavenly Father and a welcome that far surpasses any we've experienced in this life.

questions to ponder . . .

1. What does "going home" mean to you? What images does it bring to mind?

2. What do you think heaven will be like?

3. How does realizing that your citizenship is in heaven affect the way you see the world? Your life? Your circumstances?

4. How does it affect the way you live?

time in prayer . . .

Thank God for the journey, for the process. Thank him for the things he is teaching and showing you along the way and for the opportunity to go home to heaven—to be with him. Ask God to help you through today. Ask him to help you keep your eyes on him and enjoy the journey.

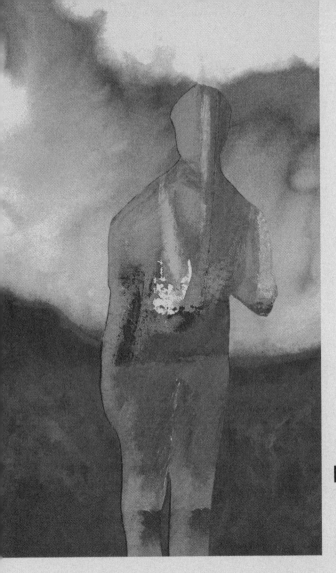

7

no more pretending

no more pretending

i can look good when i want to
i know the right things to say
i cover up what i don't want You to see
but You see it anyway
maybe i think i can fool You
maybe i'm fooling myself
i want to change but i don't know how
and i need Your help

(Chorus)
no more pretending
no more pretending
Lord, i know i need to tell you the truth tonight
everything is not all right in my life
and i need You like never before
i don't want to pretend anymore

i'm tired of hiding my weakness
i'm tired of trying to look strong
i don't want to say that everything's fine
when there's so much that's wrong
tell me again that You love me
though it's more than my heart understands
and i will lay down my disguises
and show You who i am

(Chorus)

Kyle and I sat in a BMG writer's room and chatted for two hours. We talked about our lives, our families, and our careers. Eventually, late in the afternoon, we got around to trying to write a song. I figured we wouldn't get that much done, since it was getting so late, but hoped we could get started on an idea. I shared my longing to write a song about being honest. Kyle seemed interested, so we tossed around the idea. Near the end of our session, Kyle asked if he could play me a chorus. He said it was something he had written awhile back at a weekend retreat. When I heard the chorus to "No More Pretending," I knew it was exactly what I had wanted to say. I asked whether he minded if I tried to write some verses. He had no objections.

We parted ways, and I couldn't wait to get home. I walked in the door and went straight to the keyboard. I poured out my heart, simply wrote down what I was feeling at the time about the issues the Lord was wrestling with in my life. A couple of weeks later, Kyle and I got back together and tightened up the lyric. Our aim was to write an honest song about honesty. And, I think, with God's help, we did.

no more pretending

I can pretend to be something I'm not—but what good does it do?

- Search me, O God, and know my heart;
  test me and know my anxious thoughts.
  See if there is any offensive way in me, and
  lead me in the way everlasting.

  Psalm 139:23–24

who am i fooling?

I woke up this morning, took a shower, got dressed, put some gel in my hair, ate a little breakfast, brushed my teeth, and I was just about ready to go. One last look in the mirror, a kiss for my wife, and off I went. You too?

I know I'm sometimes too concerned with my appearance. The thing that scares me even more is that I worry about what other people will think. It isn't just the clothes. I think that if I look the right way and say the right things people will like me. When I was in high school, I hung out with the "cool" crowd. In college, I pretended to know what I wanted to do in life. And at church, I pretended I had no problems. I needed to look as if I had it together—

or what would they think? If they knew what was really going on, they'd never accept me. I told myself these lies for a long time; I still struggle with them.

Honesty.

Who am I trying to fool? Myself? Those around me? God? Sometimes it seems like all three. Why do I do it? I do it because I'm afraid: I want to be accepted and I want to be loved, and I'm afraid I won't get the acceptance I crave if I'm honest. I'm afraid *I* won't be able to accept myself, I'm afraid *others* won't accept me, and I'm certainly afraid a perfect *God* won't accept me.

I can pretend to be something I'm not—but what good does it do?

So I'm trying to be honest—with myself, with God, and with others. And my efforts must begin with *myself*. I must take a hard look at my life, my desires, and my motivations. I don't always like what I see. I struggle with so much. God often has to show me things about myself—feelings, thoughts, prejudices—that I didn't even know existed! Many times I find I struggle with the same old sin—you know the one you bring before the Lord and say, "Father . . . I did it again." I know God wants to change these things, but I've got to be honest about them first. I'm *far* from having it all together, but I'm trying.

Next, I've got to be honest with *God*. But honesty with God has always perplexed me. Somehow I think I can hide things from him, but he is all-knowing and sees right through my disguises. "The Lord does not look at the things man looks at. Man looks at the outward appearance, but the Lord looks at the heart" (1 Samuel 16:7). Being honest with God usually involves confession, because if I am trying to hide something, that something is usually sin in my life. God wants to change these areas and make me more like him, but I need to acknowledge the sin, lay it before him, and ask for forgiveness. It's not always easy, but there is a freedom that results from this kind of honesty.

Freedom from the hiding.

Freedom from the secrets.

Freedom from the sin.

It's also important to be honest with *others*. Everyone struggles with something. I haven't met any perfect people—at least not yet. We need to stick together, pray for each other, and keep each other accountable. We are not alone. The more I talk to others about my struggles and my sins, the more I realize that others are struggling too. We all need help—and we all need God.

Try to find a close friend, a family member, a pastor with whom you can lay down your disguises and be real. Search for someone you can trust—someone you feel safe with. Share your struggles, your dreams, your insecurities, your joys, and your sins. Pray for each other. I can't guarantee that it will be easy, but the accountability that honesty brings is spiritually healthy, and it's great to have the support and prayers of others.

The love and acceptance I so desperately crave is offered freely and wholeheartedly by my heavenly Father. God's claims to love us are not merely talk, he offers *proof*: "But God demonstrates his own love for us in this: While we were still sinners, Christ died for us" (Romans 5:8). God gave the ultimate sacrifice—his own Son—and he did it while I was still estranged from him. God loves me—the sinner.

I guess honesty is a daily battle. It's the fight to lay down the facade and show ourselves, God, and those around us who we really are. As scary as it is, we can rest in the fact that we have a God who loves us—without our disguises.

questions to ponder . . .

1. Though the outside of your life may look good, what's going on inside?

2. Who do you have the most trouble being honest with—yourself, God, others? Why?

3. What do you find yourself doing to gain the acceptance of others?

4. What are the things you struggle with? Try making a list—be honest.

time in prayer . . .

Ask the Lord to help you be honest with yourself, with him, and with those around you. Ask him to help you lay down your disguises. Bring each item on your struggle list before him and ask for help. Ask him to shine his light on your life to see if there are other areas that need changing. Thank the Lord for his unconditional love and for sending Jesus to die for your sins.

no more pretending

How am I ever going to make it through tonight?

■ My grace is sufficient for you, for my power is made perfect in weakness.

2 Corinthians 12:9

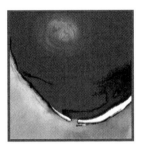

when we're weak

It was the midpoint of a three-week tour. I had been a little under the weather when I started the trip, so by the night I was to give this particular concert in California, my voice was nearly gone. I remember walking into the large church building thinking, "How am I ever going to make it through tonight?" I was tired. I was frustrated. And I could barely sing a note. I wish I could tell you that God healed my voice and that I sang better that night than ever—but that's not what happened. What I can tell you is that through the course of that evening I learned some very important lessons.

All my life I've been a singer. I am extremely grateful for the gift of music the Lord has given me. Over the years, I've caught glimpses of how the Lord works through music, and I figured that music was the way God would work through me. But that night in California, the music was almost gone. I was weak, and I didn't expect the Lord to work. But I'm thankful God is bigger than my small view of him.

That evening he worked in wonderful ways, in ways I never would have imagined. We sang some praise choruses and a few other songs. I talked a little. I cried a little. Hearts were softened, and lives were changed.

It wasn't me. It was God.

I was weak. He was strong.

My life changed that night. I came in hardhearted and worried about how stupid I was going to sound. I left humbled. There is no mistaking it: God does the real work, the life-changing kind of work—I am simply a vessel.

Paul talked a lot about weakness: "Therefore I will boast all the more gladly about my weaknesses, so that Christ's power may rest on me. That is why, for Christ's sake, I delight in weaknesses, in insults, in hardships, in persecutions, in difficulties. For when I am weak, then I am strong" (2 Corinthians 12:9–10). When we are weak, we know that we can't do it alone. When we are weak, we see our need for God. Whether it's a storm, a struggle, suffering or sickness, we know that it's God's grace and strength that bring us through—not our own.

Take a look at your life. What are some of your weaknesses? How might the Lord want to use those for his glory? Our God made us the way we are—including all our strengths and weaknesses—and everyone of us is different. We often see how he uses our strengths, but we fail to recognize that he may work through our weakness. Paul said, "If I must boast, I will boast of the things that show my weakness" (2 Corinthians 11:30). What a way to look at life! Not only does our weakness remind us of our need for God, but it clears the way for others to see him as well. When we are out of the way, he may be seen that much clearer. That night in California, there wasn't much of me left to see or hear, but God was alive and well . . . and working.

questions to ponder . . .

1. When have you been weak?

2. In what ways have you witnessed God's strength when you were weak?

3. What do you think Paul means when he talks about boasting of the things that show weakness?

time in prayer . . .

Thank God for his perfect power and strength. Thank him that he is strong when you are weak. Then present your weaknesses before him. Ask that his will be done and that he be glorified.

8

love me enough

love me enough

there's a fire in my heart
a flame burning bright
with desire every day
to be more like Christ
i want to stay pure in every way
but if there comes a time when it seems that i stray

(Chorus)
i hope you love me enough
to tell me i'm wrong
for loving correction
only helps make me strong
speaking truth in love
to a good friend is tough
but i hope, yes i hope
that you love me enough

i'm sure i'll make some excuses
for the way that i've been
when you show me how
God's Word exposes my sin
when i see that i fail to live as i should
i know it will hurt but still for my good

(Chorus)

for as iron sharpens iron
so let it be with one another
faithful are the wounds
of a sister or a brother who will . . .

(Chorus)

■ THE STORY BEHIND THE SONG

Although it was almost three years ago, I clearly remember the first day I read the words to "Love Me Enough." Tony Wood told me he had a lyric I might like and asked if I would read it. I went by my publisher's office, where Tony had taped the lyric on the door. Sitting in my car, I read through the words, and I was totally enthralled by this brilliant lyric about accountability. Loving someone enough to tell him he is wrong is a tough thing. Speaking the truth in love is a difficult and delicate art.

I started working on the music when I got home. Over time, this music has gone through many changes. At first, the music was uptempo, but the lyric didn't quite ring true with that kind of music. So I rewrote it as a ballad. About two years later we finally put it on tape, and we settled on something in-between for the record. However, when I sing this song live, I tend to lean more toward the ballad—that version still moves me the most.

love me enough

What does loving

God look like?

■ "Love the Lord your God with all your heart and with all your soul and with all your mind." This is the first and greatest commandment. And the second is like it: "Love your neighbor as yourself."

Matthew 22:37–39

loving like Jesus loved

I want to be like Jesus; I want to love like he loved. But loving others is no easy task. Even though Jesus teaches us how to love by his example, it's still tough. Sometimes we don't even know what love is.

> This is how we know what love is: Jesus Christ laid down his life for us. And we ought to lay down our lives for our brothers. If anyone has material possessions and sees his brother in need but has no pity on him, how can the love of God be in him? Dear children, let us not love with words or tongue but with actions and in truth. (1 John 3:16–18)

Loving others is not merely saying the words. Sometimes we have to get our hands dirty. Maybe loving our neighbor means listening when someone needs to be heard. Maybe it means buying a sandwich for someone who can't afford one. Maybe it means helping out a neighbor financially or sharing our possessions. Maybe loving means praying for a friend—or an enemy. Love can look different in different situations.

Although love's expression will vary, one thing will never change—the commandment to love. And no one falls outside the boundaries of our "debt" to love. "Let no debt remain outstanding, except the continuing debt to love one another, for he who loves his fellowman has fulfilled the law" (Romans 13:8). We are not excused from loving anyone.

Jesus pushes us to the limit when he says, "You have heard that it was said, 'Love your neighbor and hate your enemy.' But I tell you: Love your enemies and pray for those who persecute you" (Matthew 5:43–44). Whoa! It's hard enough to love the people we like, but love our enemies? Who are our enemies? Okay, so there's probably no one out to kill us, but what about people who cut us off in traffic or take our parking spaces? What about people who deliberately lie to us, hurt us, or talk behind our backs? What about them?

Who are you angry with? Who has hurt you? Try praying for these people—not that God will get them back for what they did to you, but for the state of their hearts or their circumstances. Carry them before our forgiving God and ask him to forgive them as he teaches you how to do the same. This is just one way we can begin to love our enemies.

It's not so hard to understand why loving others is difficult, but loving God isn't always easy either. Jesus says we are to love God with our whole heart, soul, and mind—with everything we have and are. But what does loving God look like? "If you love me, you will obey what I command" (John 14:15). *Loving* God means *obeying* God. It means making life changes; it means putting his will above our own; it means living sacrificially. It's easy to say, "I love God"; it's not so simple to live.

As the author of love and as our creator, God calls us to love him and those around us:

> We love because he first loved us. (1 John 4:19)

> Since God so loved us, we also ought to love one another. (1 John 4:11)

> Let us love one another, for love comes from God. (1 John 4:7)

When I remember how much the God of the universe loves me, I am compelled to love—to follow him and obey his commands. God loves us perfectly. There is no greater love. We couldn't love without being loved—we wouldn't know how. He loves us so that we might share the love we've found in him.

I doubt it will ever be easy to fully love God and to truly love my neighbors. It is a large and difficult task and one I will always need to work on. I know I will need God's strength and grace. But God is good. He gives us not only his grace and strength, but also the best example of love known to mankind—his love for us.

questions to ponder . . .

1. Who are your neighbors? What are some tangible ways to love them?

2. How is love a "duty"? How does that concept of love fit your current concept?

3. Who are your enemies? What does it look like to love them?

4. What life changes do you need to make to express your love to God in obedience to him?

time in prayer . . .

Thank God for the commandment to love. Ask God to help you to love him better. Ask him to show you who your neighbors are and to bring to mind some outcasts and enemies. Ask him to help you love them well. Thank God for his grace.

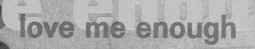
Can my friendships survive honesty?

As iron sharpens iron, so one man sharpens another.

Proverbs 27:17

a good friend

I met Rodi in college. I think we were interested in the same girl for a while and actually met at her sorority house. Soon after, we began bumping into each other in the oddest places. We ran into each other on the third floor of the school music building when neither of us had any reason to be up there. The next day we crossed paths in a bathroom. On and off campus, we kept seeing each other—weird for two people who had just met. After a few days in a row of these strange meetings, we wondered if God was trying to tell us something. We took the next logical step and had ice cream together. (A lot can be learned over a good scoop of ice cream.) We each asked questions and told stories, and we began to get to know one another.

A few months later we were, separately, presented with an opportunity to travel to Washington, D.C., to be a part of a student leadership conference. We both decided to go, and we spent a week attending seminars, talking about life, and praying together.

At one of those meetings, we were challenged to find someone with whom to commit to a deep friendship. Rodi and I thought, talked, and prayed about it. We hadn't known each other all that long, but the circumstances of our relationship were already unexplainable, so we decided to pursue a commitment to friendship—a commitment to love one another and be accountable to each other.

As the months passed, our friendship deepened. We continued to get to know each other better—the good and the bad. I gave Rodi permission to tell me when I was wrong or headed down a dangerous path. He did the same for me.

It's tough to actually tell a friend he's wrong. What will he think? What will he do? Will the friendship last? Over the years, our friendship has not only lasted but has become stronger. I don't make a major decision without his input. We talk about music, our prayer lives, marriage; we even discussed the writing of this book. He knows my strengths and weaknesses, and how and where I'm tempted. He is a sounding board. He checks my motivations. Rodi and I are committed to this relationship for life. We want to help each other become more like Christ and deepen our relationship with him.

I make mistakes; sometimes I can see them, but sometimes I cannot. Rodi knows me well enough to ask the tough questions. Sometimes he simply confirms that I've made a mistake, and other times he shines a light into an area where I can't see that I'm stumbling. He's a good friend. I can easily say that I know the Lord better because of him.

The Scriptures say to "spur one another on toward love and good deeds" (Hebrews 10:24). I don't know about you, but the idea of being "spurred" doesn't sound too enjoyable, and "speaking the truth in love" (Ephesians 4:15) is not always easy. But being accountable to one another is important. If the goal is to deepen our relationship with Christ and to get to know him better and if the truth is spoken with gentleness and in love, then correction really can help us become stronger.

If you have an accountability relationship with someone, may I encourage you to continue to pursue and deepen it. And if not, may I strongly suggest that you seek to find someone you trust and can feel comfortable being honest with. It's worth the time. It's worth the effort. And it's worth the risk.

Rodi and I live in different parts of the country now, but our relationship is still growing. We saw each other recently in California, and as usual, it seemed as if we'd never missed a beat. Our communication now is mainly through e-mail or over the phone, but we still love each other, and we still ask the tough questions. As I think back to those "coincidental" meetings and our bowls of ice cream years ago, and as I reflect on the friendship that has developed, it's easy to see that God knew exactly what he was doing.

questions to ponder . . .

1. Who are your good friends? How much do they know about you—your struggles, your weaknesses?

2. Are you accountable to someone? Is anyone accountable to you? If not, is there a person in your life with whom you could begin such a relationship?

3. What can you do to initiate a relationship of accountability?

time in prayer . . .

Thank God for your relationships. Thank him for the gift of friendship. Thank him for the people in your life who ask you the tough questions. Ask him to deepen your relationships with him and your friends. Ask him for wisdom on how to speak the truth in love.

9

wiser

wiser

You change me like the seasons
like it's second nature to You
You gave my heart a reason
to believe that some things are still true
in a world where people deal dirty hands
just to see You cry
You show me Your power
that heals the wounds inside

(Chorus)
now i'm wiser
that i know You
i'm better than i was
i'm dancing on a wire
shouting poetry of love
i'm wiser, i am wiser
i'm wiser
because of You

if You knew the evolution
that brought me to this place
You would know why my emotions
are stuck into this state
of an insane insanity
that embraces all You are
don't ask me to explain it
i don't know where to start

(Chorus)

Your faith in me
strips me of my pride
Your love breathes an honesty
that brings my soul to life

Ty Lacy, Dan Muckala, Tim Putnam, Scott Cassettari

■ THE STORY BEHIND THE SONG

Ty Lacy and I had just finished writing a song. Sometimes, at the end of our writing time together, we'll play each other some of the new things we've written. He put a cassette in the tape machine and "Wiser" started playing. I was intrigued by it musically, and I related to the lyric. I asked him to play it again. As I heard the song for the second time, I began to realize I wanted to sing the words to both the Lord and Katy. I love them both.

I am wiser because I know God, and I'm trying to grow in my relationship with him. And I am wiser because of my wife. I continue to learn much from watching and listening to her.

This song, for me, was a way to say I love you and thank you. Sometimes, when I hear it or sing it, I think about my wife. And other times I am mindful of and grateful for my relationship with a holy living God.

Ty, Dan, Tim, and I collaborated to write a great song. It is an honor to be able to record and sing it. "Wiser" continues to speak truth about and into my life—and I hope into yours as well.

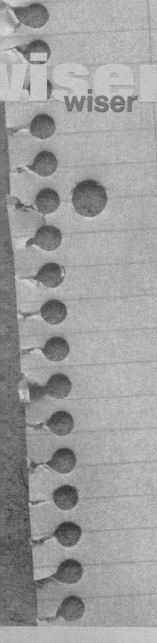

How can she love me in spite of my selfishness?

■ She speaks with wisdom, and faithful instruction is on her tongue.

Psalm 36:5

a wise woman

My wife, Katherine Marie Sillers, is a truly amazing woman. We first met at a wedding reception, and her beauty, poise, and personality absolutely *wowed* me. We were married in July of 1994. She loves God, she loves people, and she loves me. And in our first three years of marriage, she has taught me more about God than I could have ever dreamed. Here is some of what Katy has taught me.

She's shown me what grace looks like. God's grace has always been tough for me to grasp. I believe in my head that it is by his grace that I am saved, but the practical application of that concept seems to elude me. Over the years, Katy has taught me what grace looks like when lived out in real life. I've made some mistakes in this marriage, and I know I've said and done some things that have hurt Katy badly. But throughout, and in spite of, my selfishness and stupidity, her love has remained true and faithful.

Katy is the closest thing to unconditional love I have ever experienced. Regardless of what I do or don't do, she has chosen to love me. (Bless her heart.) I've always believed that God loves us unconditionally, but to see someone practice that kind of love toward me has helped me understand it better. God loves us regardless of what we do or don't do. He loves us far more than we deserve. And Katy loves me that way too.

Katy reminds me to seek God. When I'm worried, Katy points me in the direction of a Father who takes care of his children. When my mind is cluttered, confused, or focused on the wrong things, she reminds me to seek God. "But seek first his kingdom and his righteousness, and all these things will be given to you as well. Therefore do not worry about tomorrow, for tomorrow will worry about itself" (Matthew 6:33–34).

Katy has taught me more about serving others. Because Katy has shown me grace and unconditional love and because she continues to help me focus on God, I, in turn, want to love and serve Katy better. Her other-minded prayers have taught me to be less selfish, and I've learned to love others better by watching her care for those around her.

Can you think of someone who has taught you something about, or brought you closer to, God? A spouse? A friend? A teacher? Our heavenly Father has placed us on this earth together for many reasons. I believe one of those reasons is so we can learn from one another—that we might ultimately grow closer to God. You never know whom he will use. It may be someone close to you or someone you've just met. It may be a person who is in your life for only a season. Keep your eyes and ears open; stay alert; look and listen for what the Lord may be trying to show you.

I've learned a lot from Katy and look forward to learning and growing much more over the years. She is a wonderful woman, and I feel fortunate that we get to spend our lives with each other. The Lord has used her mightily in my life, and he continues to draw us closer together. Katy is truly a gift from God, and I am wiser because of her.

questions to ponder . . .

1. What valuable things have you learned about God from another person? Who? How did he or she teach you?

2. What attributes or attitudes can you see in those around you that you might learn?

3. What can others learn about God through you?

time in prayer . . .

Thank God for the people he's placed in your life to help you learn—your parents, friends, mentors. Ask God to help you know him and understand him better. Ask God to help you see him in the people around you. Ask him to make you into a vessel through which he is seen.

wiser

wiser

I've known the Lord for ten years now. Am I any wiser?

■ Blessed is the man who finds wisdom, the man who gains understanding, for she is more profitable than silver and yields better returns than gold.

Proverbs 3:13–14

am i wiser?

I've known the Lord Jesus Christ as my personal Lord and Savior for ten years now. Am I any wiser? I suppose so. I have encountered God, studied Scripture, learned from experience, and learned from others. I think I understand a bit more about who God is, and I hope our relationship is growing.

But the funny thing is—what wisdom I have gained continues to reveal how much I don't know. Maybe my relationship with God has grown, but I now realize that I have much farther to go than I originally thought. The more I understand, the more I see I don't understand. Wisdom creates more questions. The more I learn, the more questions I have. What have I learned?

I understand better what a sinner I am. I am not just an individual who occasionally sins; I am a sinner—and I am confident there are areas of sin in my life that I still don't even know are there.

I am more aware of my need for a Savior—because I am more aware of my sin. I just can't seem to get things right, no matter how hard I try. I will never be good enough to earn God's love—it's not possible. I need a Savior. I need Jesus. God's love for me—for us—is greater than I ever imagined. As I see my own sin, Jesus' death on the cross becomes that much more incredible.

I'm learning that my walk with God is less like religion and more like a relationship. As a youngster, I grew up with a very legalistic view of God—the Big Eye in the sky. He was always watching and waiting to catch me. I had to do this, and I mustn't do that. And if I blew it, watch out! I carried a lot of this thinking over into my adult relationship with God. I felt that if I went to church every week and had consistent quiet times, I was a better Christian. I thought God would like me more . . . love me more. But as I get to know the Lord better and as I continue to learn about grace, I realize that although quiet times and church can be great things, they don't score points for me in God's eyes. He loves me, in Christ, the way I am. I want my quiet times to help me know the Lord more and deepen our relationship—not move me up a few notches in my Christian "standing." And I want to attend church out of a desire to worship a living God and a longing to serve him—not out of a need to fill a quota.

I'm learning that I don't have all the answers. I'm just beginning to ask the questions. Some things I used to see as black and white are starting to have color. And I'm discovering that some things I thought were cut and dry are still a little wet. I thought I had most things figured out, but I'm beginning to see that I've only scratched the surface. There's so much I don't know. There's so much I don't understand.

God is awesome. He is mysterious. He is omniscient. And as incredible as it may seem, he loves us! He loves us right where we are. He loves us as we try to comprehend all that he is; he loves us as we struggle as sinners saved by his grace; and he loves us as we begin to realize that we really don't understand all that much.

So, it's been ten years, yet sometimes it seems as if I know less than I did a decade ago. I wonder what the next ten will be like. What will I learn? What will the Great Teacher reveal? One thing is sure—I know I have a long way to go. Am I wiser? Sure. But maybe it's because I realize that I am still a fool.

questions to ponder . . .

1. What were you like when you first met Jesus?

2. How have you grown?

3. What have you learned?

4. What questions do you still have?

5. Where can you still grow?

time in prayer . . .

Thank God for revealing himself. Thank him for the opportunity to know him and walk with him and for the things he has taught you and the ways he has changed you. Ask God for wisdom, discernment, and understanding. Ask him to continue the work he has begun in you and bring it to completion.

10

hope has a way

hope has a way

hey you, with your fist balled up tight
against your brother
hey you, with the hate in your heart
for another
it's no surprise that you struggle inside
playing tug-o-war with your stubborn pride, remember

hope has a way
of breaking through walls
and bridging the gap between us all
there isn't a problem
too great or too small
hope has a way, hope has a way

how come we throw words like stones
against each other
and how long before we begin to love
one another

haven't we learned from the mistakes we've made
that without forgiveness, there is no change, but

let's not forget that what binds us is greater
than anything that keeps us apart
we're all the children of the same loving Father
let us stand together serving heart to heart

Scott Krippayne, Tony Wood and Ty Lacy
© 1996 BMG Songs, Inc. (ASCAP), Above The Rim Music (ASCAP) and Shepherd's Fold
Music (BMI). All rights on behalf of Above The Rim Music administered by BMG Songs, Inc.
(ASCAP)

■ THE STORY BEHIND THE SONG

Katy and I invited Ty to come over for dinner. We thought we'd catch a movie and then come back and have a meal. Funny how plans change. On the way to our apartment, Ty came up with the chorus idea for "Hope Has a Way." So when he got to our apartment, he was ready to work. We sat down at the keyboard and began to tighten up the chorus. We worked on the first verse for a while and then called it a night. (I think we actually made the movie.)

The next week we called Tony and asked if he would help finish the song. He accepted the challenge. Piece by piece the song fell into place. We wrote and rewrote until we were satisfied.

The completed song deals with racial, social, and denominational issues. The bridge reminds us that we are all children of God and that we should work together to break down the walls that separate us and build bridges across our differences. And the hope we find in Jesus Christ offers a way to do just that.

Do I dare to
hope in what
I can't see?

■ Be strong and take heart, all you who hope
in the Lord.

Psalm 31:24

where is your hope?

Hope may be why you got out of bed this morning—a hope that today would be better than yesterday. And even if today wasn't what you'd hoped, you hope tomorrow will be.

Hope.

It's a strange thing.

It's a powerful thing.

Some people hope for great wealth or power. Others hope to find someone who loves them. Some hope to pass that math test on Friday. And others just hope to make it through the day. What do you hope for?

Hope keeps us going. It gives us a reason to try, try, and

try again. Hope gives us a reason to live. We may get discouraged if time and time again our hopes are not realized. And if this disappointment and discouragement continue, we may head down a road toward despair—until we lose all hope. Hopelessness is a scary and dangerous place. But even for those who feel they have lost all hope, there is a hope that remains—a different kind of hope—hope in Jesus Christ.

Now, the hope found in Jesus is not the same as hoping you'll pass your math test. If you don't know how to work the math equations, your foundation for hope is shaky at best. Hope in Jesus is much more than a grasping at straws, much more than a "hope against hope"; it is a firm expectation that the promises of Christ are true. It is more a looking forward to a future reality than a "wishing upon a star" that perhaps a dream will come true. As Christians, our hope is in things as yet unseen: "Hope that is seen is no hope at all. Who hopes for what he already has? But if we hope for what we do not yet have, we wait for it patiently" (Romans 8:24–25). We wait . . . patiently. We have faith. And we keep believing. Our hope in Christ *will* one day be realized. The hope of Christ is the hope of *salvation*—a promise straight from the Word of God.

When we place our trust in Christ, we have an eternal hope. Our hope is founded in the grace of God, through his Son, Jesus, who saves us and offers us the hope of heaven—everlasting life. Even when we have a lousy day—or a lousy year—even when we make mistakes or unwise choices, even when our earthly "hopes" are shattered, we long for and wait for a time and a place where the pain and struggles are no more. We have faith . . . and we hope. There will still be suffering here on earth; we will still struggle, but we look forward to the realization of eternal hope.

If things are going well, continue to hope in the Lord your God. And if things are crazy, hang on tight. No matter how tough things get, no matter how discouraged you may become, hold on to hope. "We have this hope as an anchor for the soul, firm and secure" (Hebrews 6:19). Hold on to a hope that is secure—a hope that will not let you down—the hope of Christ.

And tomorrow morning if you wake up and need a reason to get out of bed, find something to believe in, someone to put your faith in, and something to hope for. May I suggest Jesus Christ?

questions to ponder . . .

1. What things do you hope for?

2. Have you ever felt discouraged because your hopes were not fulfilled? When?

3. What is the difference between worldly hope and eternal hope?

4. How can eternal hope help you get through times when your earthly dreams are shattered?

time in prayer . . .

Thank God for a hope you can hold on to—for the hope that is found in his Son, Jesus. Thank him for the hope of salvation and everlasting life. Ask God to increase your patience and strengthen your faith as you live each day.

Why do we tend to focus on our differences when we have so much common ground?

■ There is one body and one Spirit—just as you were called to one hope when you were called—one Lord, one faith, one baptism; one God and Father of all, who is over all and through all and in all.

Ephesians 4:4–6

one Lord

Why do we tend to focus on our differences when we have so much common ground? Why do we often see the things that separate us rather than the things that bring us together? Why do we raise our fists in anger when we are called to love? What I'm speaking of may surprise you. I'm talking about the church—the body of Christ.

So often we try to pull apart what God intends to be unified. Listen as Paul addresses the Romans: "May the God who gives endurance and encouragement give you a spirit of unity among yourselves as you follow Christ Jesus, so that with one heart and mouth you may glorify the God and Father of our Lord Jesus Christ" (Romans

15:5–6). We are to work together toward a common goal—the goal of becoming more like Christ. We are to speak with "one heart and mouth"—in order to glorify God.

Paul goes on to say, "Accept one another, then, just as Christ accepted you, in order to bring praise to God" (Romans 15:7). We may disagree, and we may have differences, but we can accept one another anyway. None of us is perfect. Not one person, not one church has a flawless theology or interpretation of the Bible. We are flawed individuals—flawed in our understanding of Scripture and flawed in our practical life application of Scripture. We are sinners. But we are sinners saved by the grace of God and accepted by Jesus Christ; and since this is true, we should accept one another.

Sometimes we allow race or social class to divide us; but, here again, we are gravely wrong.

> Here there is no Greek or Jew, circumcised or uncircumcised, barbarian, Scythian, slave or free, but Christ is all, and is in all. Therefore, as God's chosen people, holy and dearly loved, clothe yourselves with compassion, kindness, humility, gentleness, and patience. Bear with each other and forgive whatever grievances you may have against one another. Forgive as the Lord forgave you. And over all these virtues put on love, which binds them all together in perfect unity. Let the peace of Christ rule in your hearts, since as members of one body you were called to peace. (Colossians 3:11–15)

We are members of one body under the lordship of Jesus Christ, and we all have at least two things in common: we are all sinners, and we all need Jesus. That's a good place to start. Let's allow our hope in Christ to build bridges across our differences. Let's work together to break down the walls that divide us. Our desire to follow Christ and our hope in him can be the common ground on which we stand.

"There are many parts, but one body" (1 Corinthians 12:20). *You* are a part of the body. *I* am a part as well. *We* are the body of Christ. We are the church: we are unique individuals coming together to form one body. We bring different strengths, different weaknesses, different doctrines, and different agendas. We may come from different cultures. But we are all children of God. And we have one hope—the hope of Christ. Let's build one another up instead of tearing each other down. Let's help instead of hurt. Let's love one another well as we strive to follow our one Lord and Savior, Jesus Christ.

questions to ponder . . .

1. Name some fellow believers with whom you differ or disagree. In what ways is your thinking or practice different?

2. What do you have in common?

3. What steps can you take to work through your differences?

time in prayer . . .

Thank God for his church. Thank him for sending his Son, Jesus. Thank him for the common ground we have in Christ. Ask him to help you be an active member of the body. Ask him to help you break down walls and build bridges.

11

**sometimes He
calms the storm**

sometimes He calms the storm

all who sail the sea of faith
find out before too long
how quickly blue skies can grow dark
and gentle winds grow strong
suddenly fear is like white water
pounding on the soul
but still we sail on knowing
that our Lord is in control

sometimes He calms the storm
with a whispered "peace be still"
He can settle any sea
but it doesn't mean He will
sometimes He holds us close
and lets the wind and waves go wild
sometimes He calms the storm
and other times He calms His child

He has a reason for each trial
that we pass through in life
and though we're shaken
we cannot be pulled apart from Christ
no matter how the driving rain beats down
on those who hold to faith
a heart of trust will always
be a quiet peaceful place

Tony Wood and Kevin Stokes
© 1995 BMG Songs, Inc. (ASCAP) and Careers-BMG Music Publishing, Inc. (BMI)

Sometimes the songwriters and publishers around town get together to play songs for the record companies who are looking. One of these days was coming up, and Tony Wood asked if I would be willing to learn a song he had written and play it at the meeting. "Sure, why not," The name of the song was "Sometimes He Calms the Storm."

We had just started selecting songs for my first record, and I knew from the moment I heard this one that it was great. But I wanted to write everything on this record, so I really wasn't open to outside songs. Thankfully, John Mays, an executive at Word, was at that meeting when I sang Tony's song. He loved it and thought it would be great for the record. Like I said before, I really liked the song, but I was being selfish. I'm glad John was persistent, and I'm grateful that God changed my attitude.

"Sometimes He Calms the Storm" is truly an amazing song, and I was fortunate to be able to record it. Over the past couple of years, I've heard countless stories of how the Lord has used the song in people's lives. He has used it in my life as well.

Thank you Tony and Kevin for giving us a wonderful song.

sometimes He calms the storm

What kind of man is this?

> He stilled the storm to a whisper; the waves of the sea were hushed.
>
> Psalm 107:29

he is able

Then he got into the boat and his disciples followed him. Without warning, a furious storm came up on the lake, so that the waves swept over the boat. But Jesus was sleeping. The disciples went and woke him, saying, "Lord, save us! We're going to drown!"

He replied, "You of little faith, why are you so afraid?" Then he got up and rebuked the wind and the waves, and it was completely calm.

The men were amazed and asked, "What kind of man is this? Even the winds and the waves obey him." (Matthew 8:23–27)

Jesus calms the storm. The story appears in three of the Gospels—Matthew, Mark, and Luke. It is a powerful passage. Let's look a little closer and see what we can learn about our own lives and about God.

Let's first take a look at the storm. The Bible says the storm came up "without warning." Like the weather, the storms in our lives sometimes take us by surprise. They are frequently unpredictable and seldom come at opportune times. And often, we're unprepared for what they bring.

The storm in this passage is described as "furious"— "the waves swept over the boat." This was no annoying drizzle or light breeze—this was a wind-gusting, wave-building, boat-drenching storm. And sometimes we experience similar storms—the kind that can turn our lives upside down.

I think it's important to note that this storm fell upon men who were following Jesus. Following Christ doesn't assure us that we won't run into trouble. The Christian life is not always easy—it's not always "storm free." The disciples certainly went through them, and so will we.

Let's look now at the response of the disciples. They were afraid for their lives and thought they might drown. So they woke Jesus. They went to their Lord. They knew who to turn to in the midst of the storm. I wonder how long they waited. Did they go wake Jesus immediately, or did they try to battle the storm for a while on their own? I'm not sure, but we do know they went to Jesus hoping he would save them.

What was Jesus' response? After a brief rebuke of their lack of faith, he turned his attention to the storm and demonstrated his control. He "rebuked the wind and the waves" and completely calmed the storm. The wind and waves obeyed him. The Lord had power over the storm.

Our Lord also has power over the storms of our lives. He is in control and able to calm any storm. Even when the storms of life are raging, terrifying, and unpredictable— God is in control. The one who settled the sea and calmed the storm years ago is able to do the same in our lives today.

questions to ponder . . .

1. What storms have you been through in your life?

2. How did you respond to the storm? Were you afraid?

3. Who did you turn to for help?

time in prayer . . .

Thank God for being in control and for being able to calm the storms of life. Ask him to help you turn to him when you're going through trouble, trials, or storms.

the storm

sometimes He calms the storm

If God has the power to calm the storms of life, why doesn't he?

■ Consider it pure joy, my brothers, whenever you face trials of many kinds, because you know that the testing of your faith develops perseverance. Perseverance must finish its work so that you may be mature and complete, not lacking anything.

James 1:2–4

he is God

God does not always calm the storms in our lives. His timing may be different from ours. He most certainly is in control and has the power to calm any storm, but may not always respond the way we want him to or the way we think he should. But we must remember that he is God—we are not. He sees a bigger picture than we do.

Let's look again at the disciples' dilemma (Matthew 8:23–27). The storm was in full force, and they went to Jesus for help—they wanted him to save them. The disciples were afraid they might drown—they were afraid for their lives. And what did Jesus do? He talked to them. He addressed their "little faith"; he inquired about their fear.

If I were a disciple on that boat, I would be scared to death and dumbfounded. Waves were washing over the boat and Jesus wanted to talk about their lack of faith! Unbelievable.

This was a crisis—at least the disciples saw it as a crisis. Yet Jesus spoke first, *then* got up, and *then* calmed the storm. Why did he wait? He could have calmed the storm immediately and then talked. What was his agenda? Was there a larger plan?

If we look at our own lives, we can see that our Lord doesn't always calm the storms when we might want him to. Sometimes, it seems, he doesn't do anything. If God has the power to calm the storms of life, why doesn't he? I don't know for sure, but there are a few possibilities.

God may want to teach us perseverence—how to press on through trials and tough times and have faith that he is in control. God knows that life will be full of storms of all kinds and that the ability to persevere is an important quality.

Maybe God allows the storms to continue so that he might increase our faith. This process will not be an easy one; it will require the *testing* of our faith. God wants to build in us a faith that is able to respond with a solid "Yes!" when he asks, "Do you trust me?"—regardless of the circumstance or situation.

Also, when the storms of life are raging, we are likely to turn to God because that is when we realize just how helpless we are. He desires that we look to him, that we follow him, and that we trust him. When life is going smoothly, we sometimes think we're standing on our own, but when the storms rise up, we remember our need for God.

Or, God may want to show us that he is our refuge in the midst of the storm. He may be teaching us that he is trustworthy and will never let us go—no matter how hopeless things may seem.

And maybe, just maybe, it's not even a question of why the storms continue. Maybe the question is, "What now, Lord?" What do you want to teach me? Where do you want to take me? How do you want to mold me? I hope I will learn to look at the storms of life and ask, "How do you want to use this, Lord?"

God is in control, he will always do what is best, and he will be glorified. He may calm the storms, he may let them continue, but he is God and we are not. He allows us to lean on and rest in him. We are fortunate to have a God who is powerful enough to hush the winds and still the sea but tender enough to calm his children in the midst of any storm.

questions to ponder . . .

1. Think about some of the storms you've been through in life. When has God calmed them? When has he allowed them to continue?

2. Are you going through a storm now? What have you learned that will help you weather this storm better than the last?

3. Even if God doesn't calm a particular storm, will you allow him to calm you? How can you seek his peace?

4. How may God want to use it for his glory?

time in prayer . . .

Thank God for being able to calm any storm and for being a firm foundation in the midst of storms. Thank him for knowing and caring about what is best for you. Ask him to help you face the storms that may lie ahead.

12

could you believe?

could you believe?

there's a love that understands
all the pain you're going through
if you think you've been abandoned
love will still believe in you
i know it might sound like it's crazy
but tell me, tell me

(Chorus)
could you believe in a love like this
one that wants all of your heart
could you believe in a love
that will accept you as you are
could you believe

there's a love that keeps no record
of things done wrong or right
when you're weak and can't keep trying
love will not give up the fight
i know it might sound like it's crazy
but tell me, tell me

(Chorus)

and welcomes you with open arms
if this is really true then could you
could you, would you

(Chorus)

Scott Krippayne and George Cocchini
© 1997 BMG Songs, Inc. (ASCAP), Above The Rim Music (ASCAP) and Tigerback Music
(BMI) (Administered by CMI). All rights on behalf of Above The Rim Music administered by
BMG Songs, Inc. (ASCAP)

■ THE STORY BEHIND THE SONG

I met George the day he came to my apartment for a writing session. We chatted for a while, got to know each other a little, and then settled in to write. Our goal was to come up with a few good musical ideas. One of the things we came up with was the music for "Could You Believe?"

A few weeks later I embarked on a lyric direction. I started thinking about the fact that most of the songs I sing speak to those who already have a relationship with God. But sometimes, people who have never met God come to my concerts. Maybe friends encourage them to come, or maybe they just want to see what's going on. I wanted to write a song that would speak to someone who didn't know the love of Jesus, someone whose experiences with "love" had not been good, someone who had no real concept of unconditional love. I wanted to write a song about the perfect love of God without using a lot of Christian buzzwords.

The lyric of "Could You Believe?" describes some of the qualities of love that are talked about in 1 Corinthians 13 and then poses a simple question. If this kind of love really exists, could you believe in it? Could you place your belief in someone who loves you this way?

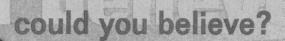

u believe?

could you believe?

How can I know God loves me?

■ Give thanks to the Lord, for he is good;
his love endures forever.

Psalm 118:1

what is love?

Love. It's a powerful word. We use it to describe how we feel. Over time, it has come to have many levels of meaning. I love pizza, and I love my wife. Same word—strong emotion—and yet I have considerably different feelings about the two. Has the word *love* lost some of its meaning? Do we use the word so much and for so many different things that it has lost some of its impact?

I'd like to reflect on love a bit—more specifically, on God's love for us. We say we believe in a God who loves us, but what does that mean? Here are a few passages to contemplate.

For the Lord is good and his love endures forever; his faithfulness continues through all generations. (Psalm 100:5)

How great is the love the Father has lavished on us, that we should be called children of God! And that is what we are! (1 John 3:1)

For God so loved the world that he gave his one and only Son, that whoever believes in him shall not perish but have eternal life. (John 3:16)

But God demonstrates his own love for us in this: While we were still sinners, Christ died for us. (Romans 5:8)

God loves us—he loves you; he loves me. Not only does he love us, he also *demonstrates* his love for us. Because we needed him to, because we were lost, he sent his Son out of the comforts of heaven to enter our planet and become a human and live among us. And when he came to live among us, we crucified him. God knew all along what the outcome would be, yet he went through with his plan because he loves us enough to give us another chance. Without the sacrifice of Jesus, our sins would forever separate us from our Father. But because God wanted to be reconciled to us, he allowed his Son—who was the only one in a position to bring us together—to pay the ultimate price: death! God sent his only begotten Son to die so that we could live. He *demonstrated* his love when he sacrificed his Son.

We hear God's love as he allows us to call him Father—he is our *Father,* he is our *heavenly* Father, and he is our *perfect* Father. And we hear God's love when he calls us his children—we are his *children,* we are *dearly loved* children, and most significantly, we are children of *God!*

His love for us is real, and he has so *much* of it to give. "The Lord is compassionate and gracious, slow to anger, abounding in love" (Psalm 103:8).

Our God has defined love. We would not know what love is if it weren't for God. "This is love, not that we loved God, but that he loved us and sent his Son as an atoning sacrifice for our sins" (1 John 4:10).

We would not be able to love God if he had not loved us—we wouldn't know how. But he does love us, and we have the opportunity to love him. He has demonstrated a greater love than the world has ever known.

We may define love in many different ways, and we may use the word for all sorts of things. We can search and study and ponder its different meanings, but the greatest definition of love is found in God's love for us. We don't deserve it, but God loves us anyway.

God loves us.

God *loves* us.

God loves *us.*

questions to ponder . . .

1. What does love mean to you? When do you use the word?

2. Have you ever felt that someone *lavished* you with love? If you have, who did it and how did that make you feel? (Look at 1 John 3:1.)

3. What special feelings and privileges exist in a father-child relationship? How is having God as *Father* different from having him only as *Lord?*

4. Is there anyone you love so much that you would allow your child to die for him or her? How much must God love you to do that for you?

time in prayer . . .

Thank God for loving you. Thank him for showing you how to love. Thank God for the example of love he gave us in his Son. Ask him to continue to teach you about his love and what it means to love others.

Does perfect love really exist?

- For I am convinced that neither death nor life, neither angels nor demons, neither the present nor the future, nor any powers, neither height nor depth, nor anything else in all creation, will be able to separate us from the love of God that is in Christ Jesus our Lord.

Romans 8:38–39

perfect love

"How could you do that to me? You said you loved me!"

Have you ever been hurt by someone who loved you? Have you ever been let down? Have you ever felt burned by love? The odds are good that, at some time or another, you have. And the odds are good that you have also delivered some of those painful blows yourself. Because, unfortunately, we are imperfect people, and we live in an imperfect world. But fortunately, we have a God who loves us perfectly and teaches us how to love others with a perfect love. When we are let down by those around us, God's love endures. And when we let others down, his love gently teaches us how to love more perfectly. Paul, in his letter to the Corinthians, describes *perfect* love.

> Love is patient, love is kind. It does not envy, it does not boast, it is not proud. It is not rude, it is not self-seeking, it is not easily angered, it keeps no record of wrongs. Love does not delight in evil but rejoices with the truth. It always protects, always trusts, always hopes, always perseveres. Love never fails. (1 Corinthians 13:4–8)

Paul gives us a model of what love *can* be—what it *should* be. *Perfect love* is unselfish: it seeks the best for the other. It chooses someone else before itself and places the needs of others in front of its own. *Perfect love* is slow to anger and doesn't hold grudges. *Perfect love* chooses compassion, mercy, and forgiveness instead of bitterness or revenge. *Perfect love* is honest, trusting, and hopeful. Imagine someone who always tells you the truth, who has unwavering faith in you, and who constantly looks for the good in you. *Perfect love* is full of goodness, kindness, and understanding. And *perfect love* does not run away; it does not give up. *Perfect love* endures and perseveres.

In this world, we will sometimes be disappointed by what we call love. There will be breakups and letdowns. The faithful can make mistakes, and the tried and true can slip and fall. Some people go through life and never meet anyone who exemplifies this perfect love. But perfect love does exist. Paul talks about it, and God demonstrates it. We have a God who loves us perfectly and much more than we deserve. He sent his Son to prove it.

questions to ponder . . .

1. Have you ever been disappointed or hurt by love? How was that love different than the love Paul talked about?

2. What does unconditional love mean to you?

3. Have you ever disappointed or hurt someone you love? How can you love that person better in the future?

4. Look again at 1 Corinthians 13:4–8. What areas of love do you need most to grow in? Choose one, and find ways to grow in love this week.

time in prayer . . .

Thank God for the biblical example of love. Thank him for loving you that way. Ask God to teach you how to learn the kind of love Paul described. Ask him to help you live it. Ask him for help in the areas you struggle with.

13

the main thing

the main thing

how do i look? what do i wear?
what will they think? why should i care?
where should i go? what should i do?
how should i live? what's it to you?

these are the questions that compete for my attention
I know there's one thing that they always fail to mention

the main thing is to keep the main thing the main thing
the main thing is to keep the main thing the main thing

who will it be? who can i trust?
how will i know if it's true love?
when is it right? when is it wrong?
why are these feelings so strong?

with all these choices i have come to this conclusion
there's only one way i can handle this confusion

Lord i know Your way will always be the best for me
so won't You help me to establish my priorities

"The Main Thing" was the first song Kyle and I ever wrote together. We started with the chorus, and after a lot of trial and error, finally found a way to set the phrase to music. It's a catchy little thing, but we wanted it to have meaning. So we chose to ask a series of questions in the verses—questions that we've all probably asked at one time or another, questions that express the confusion in our lives.

In the midst of the confusion and the questions, we need to remember what really matters. We need to keep the main thing the main thing—and that means keeping the Lord at the center of our lives and allowing everything else to fall into place around him.

It's been a joy to sing this song over the past couple of years and have people join in. My hope is that, as people leave a concert and reflect back on the evening, they will remember one thing. I hope they remember Jesus. Maybe they had a good time, maybe they saw something in a new way or even learned something, but I hope people walk away remembering the main thing—Jesus Christ.

the main thing

Why do I find it so difficult to spend quality time with God?

■ Very early in the morning, while it was still dark, Jesus got up, left the house and went off to a solitary place, where he prayed.

Mark 1:35

a quiet place

I am way too easily distracted. Sometimes it's hard for me to stay focused and on task. So many different things vie for my time and attention. This can present a real problem when I sit down to spend time with God. I can be at my desk, with my Bible open, ready to dive in, when my mind starts to wander . . . What do I have to do today? What time is it? Don't I have to be somewhere soon? I need to get a birthday card for my brother. I really should call my mom. Have we paid the bills yet? You get the idea. My mind is everywhere—except where I want it to be. It's a struggle to gain control of my thoughts, clear my head, and focus on God's Word.

Praying presents a similar dilemma. It usually takes me a good five to ten minutes of trying to pray before I really get deep into it. Sometimes it's really tough to get some unhurried, focused time with the Lord of my life.

Have you ever felt this way? Can your attention span be as short as mine? We live in a world that's geared to speed things up. Our society communicates through beepers and cellular phones; you can reach out and touch almost anyone, anytime, anywhere. Even fast food wasn't fast enough; now you can drive through and pick it up. The post office delivers "snail mail," while e-mail gets to its destination within minutes. And if you need to send a package, you can "FedEx it," so it arrives the next morning. We can probably sum up this society with the name of a credit card—*American Express* (a faster way to buy).

It's no wonder we have a tough time slowing down. We've been moving so fast for so long that it's hard to remember what it's like to be still. (I fight not to check my voicemail when we're on vacation!) It seems there's so much to get done that it's hard to take a break. But we need to slow down—we must. We need it for our physical health as well as our spiritual well-being.

It's important to spend time with God daily. Spending time with the Lord of our life can help us sort out the things that matter. When we take time to pray, we can lay our worries and our busy schedules at the feet of God and let him do what he pleases. He wants to work in our lives, but sometimes we don't even acknowledge that he exists.

Here's a little challenge (I'll try it too): tomorrow morning, when you wake up, maybe even before you take a shower, go find a quiet place and spend some time with

God. This may require getting up earlier, but I believe it's worth it. Open up his Word, and see what he has to say. Spend some time in prayer. Present your cares, your worries, and the day ahead to him. Ask him how best to use the hours in your day—seek his agenda. Allow the God of the universe to set your priorities for the day. (Let me know how it goes.)

God desires a relationship with us, but he will never force the issue. Our busy schedules may cry out for attention, but our Lord is much bigger (and more personal) than any Daytimer. We need to make time for him, to slow down, to take a break from this fast-paced world and rest in the presence of God. Let him refresh you, replenish you, and rejuvenate you. And most of all, let him love you.

questions to ponder . . .

1. What keeps you from spending time with God?

2. What time of day is best for you to spend time with God? What changes do you need to make in order to set aside some regular time?

3. What changes do you need to make in your life to help you slow down?

time in prayer . . .

Thank God for desiring and pursuing a relationship with you. Thank him for his Word. Ask him to help you prioritize your time and enable you to spend more time with him. Thank him for hearing your prayers.

Why do I put other things before God, when I know in my heart that he is supreme?

■ This is what the Lord says—Israel's King and Redeemer, the Lord Almighty: I am the first and I am the last; apart from me there is not God.

Isaiah 44:6

what's the main thing?

What's the main thing?

Is it money? Some might say so. There are people whose lives depend on the stock market. They live and die by the Dow. Money can buy some nice things, but winning the lottery isn't the solution to end all problems. Money can disappear as quickly as it appeared.

What's the main thing?

Is it power? There are people who love to be in control. They live to be the decision makers. If you have power, people take your calls, they listen to you, and they do what you say—no questions asked. The problem with longing for power is that there is always someone who has more.

What is the main thing?

Is it love? Here we have a beautiful virtue. It is a wonderful thing to love and be loved. We can love our family, our friends, and our relatives. We can care about those who are close to us. And receiving love can be almost therapeutic. The Bible says love is the greatest commandment, so it must be important. But is it the main thing? No, even love comes from somewhere else—someone else. Love comes from God. The only reason we know anything about love is that we have a God who loves us.

So what is the main thing?

I believe that *the main thing is the Lord our God.* He alone gives our lives meaning. He is the one who created it all and holds it all together. He alone is God.

Even though it's not difficult for me to acknowledge that God is the main thing, I often live my life with other priorities. God desires to be the most important part of my life; he desires to be the center of my life. And yet, at times, I place other things at the center and push the Lord toward the outside. I need to be reminded that he is the main thing. I need to continually allow him to be the Lord of all in my life.

If you know God, pursue him. Deepen your relationship with him. Make sure he is the first priority in your life. Get to know him better. Spend time with him. Dive into his Word. Find out what he cares about—what matters to him. Pray. Allow him to take control of and direct your life. Let him mold you into the person he wants you to be. And seek to love him with all of your heart, soul, mind, and strength.

And if you don't know God, may I encourage you to seek him. Open up the Bible and read about the God who created the universe. Read about the God who loves you unconditionally. Call a friend. Talk to a pastor. Ask questions. And pray. There are no right or wrong words to use when you talk to your Father; there's no right or wrong way. Just pray. Whether you think he's listening or not—he is. Seek the Lord and you will find him. The God of the Bible is alive and he wants you to know him—the main thing.

This world is full of choices: who to follow, who to trust, what's right, what's wrong, what's important, and what matters. Everyone has an opinion—some are simply louder than others. Numerous people and things will clamor for your attention. But there is a still small voice that calls you by name and and nudges your heart to worship something, someone bigger than yourself. Listen. Whether the voice is as familiar as an old friend or you're hearing it for the first time . . . listen. It is God.

questions to ponder . . .

1. What are the three most important things in your life?

2. How do these priorities line up with what matters to God?

3. What choices can you make to get your priorities more in line with God's?

time in prayer . . .

Thank God for being Lord of all. Thank him for his love for you and for knowing you by name. Ask God to help you hear his voice. Ask him to help you treat him as the main thing in your life.

14

You changed
the world

You changed the world

it's the way you've always been
and i guess you'll always be
simply loving anyone
who comes within your reach
and i can't help but think about it
every now and then
and wonder if you even know
about that moment when

(Chorus)
you changed the world
in a mighty way
you may not recall it
but i won't forget that day
when the love of God inspired you
to show me i could find the truth
in One who gave His life
so i could be free
you may not think you changed the world
but you sure changed the world for me

it's a miracle to me
how the Father sends our way
the right one at the right time
with the right words to say
i want to work in others' lives
the way you've worked in mine
and take the words i took to heart
to one heart at a time

(Chorus)

Scott Krippayne, Tony Wood and Kyle Matthews
© 1997 BMG Songs, Inc./Above The Rim Music (ASCAP) and Careers-BMG Music Publishing,
Inc./Final Four Music (BMI). All rights on behalf of Above The Rim Music are administered
by BMG Songs, Inc. (ASCAP). All rights on behalf of Final Four Music are administered by
Careers-BMG Music Publishing, Inc. (BMI)

It was my first year in town, and I was living alone in a small duplex in west Nashville. I didn't have much furniture, but I was making some friends. Tony and Kyle were two of the guys I was getting to know. They had recently finished a song lyric and wondered if I wanted to take a crack at the music. I thought, "Sure, why not?" I was trying to co-write as much as I could.

I read the lyric for the first time at home, and I started to cry. I thought about all the people who had made a difference in my life. I was amazed at how God had orchestrated it all. I picked up the phone and called my high school Bible study leader, who in my senior year had fixed a few of us breakfast every Friday morning as we learned about what it meant to be young men of God. I read him the lyric and thanked him for being willing to be used by an amazing God. Then I called the friend who had invited me to YoungLife for the first time. I read the lyric again and thanked him for his place in God's plan for molding and shaping me.

As I began to write the music, I kept these guys and others in mind—real people making a real difference. When we recorded the song nearly three years later, we didn't include the bridge—so I'll leave it with you now.

> when the need is so immense
> and you wonder
> if you really make a difference
> remember . . . you changed the world

You changed the world

Will I be faithful
to God and allow
him to work through
me in the lives of
others?

- We are therefore Christ's ambassadors, as
  though God were making his appeal
  through us.

  2 Corinthians 5:20

thank you

It was a Monday in September, at the beginning of my junior year in high school, when a couple of friends invited me to something called YoungLife. It sounded interesting. I had heard it was some sort of Christian gathering where there were cute girls and everyone sang songs. Since I had attended church all my life, the word *Christian* didn't scare me, and the girls and music were intriguing. The group was meeting just down the street from my house that night, so I decided to go. It was fun. We laughed and we sang. We heard a passage from the Bible and talked about how it related to our lives. I had a good enough time to try it again the next week . . . and the next . . . and the next.

I began to hear more about Jesus Christ and how he wanted to have a relationship with me. I started asking a few questions and found out that on Sunday nights some of the kids from YoungLife were getting together to dive a little deeper into God's Word. Before long, I started going to this "Campaigner's" group. As I listened, I heard more and more about a God who was real. There was something about the leaders too: they believed what they were saying, and they knew God personally—I could see it in their lives. They wanted to hang out with us; they cared about what was going on in our lives. At the end of the year, I had an opportunity to go to a week-long YoungLife camp in Canada. It was there that I accepted Jesus Christ as my personal Lord and Savior.

That was a major turning point in my life. It was the beginning of a new life in Christ. I now knew God loved me and sent his Son to die for me so that I could experience true, abundant life here and now and forever. The old was gone and the new had come (2 Corinthians 5:17). My life would never be the same.

As I remember that summer day in 1987, I can't help but think about the guys who invited me to YoungLife for the first time. I also think about the people who loved me and made a difference in my life, those who planted seeds, those who shared the Gospel, and those who helped build a foundation in the years that followed. All of them were being faithful to God where they were—where he had placed them. They loved him, served him, and made the most of their opportunities to share him. They talked about what was most important in their lives, and they lived it. And I am grateful. I am grateful to God for using them, and I am grateful to them for being willing to be used.

Think about your own experience. Think about your journey. How old were you when you met Jesus? Did you meet him while in school or later in life? Did the Lord use people around you? Your parents? A pastor? Your Sunday school teacher? A bus driver? A store clerk? I've heard a lot of different stories, and I'm constantly amazed at the way God works and who he uses. A recent story stands out in my mind.

There was a hitchhiker on the side of the road. A car drove past, then turned around, and finally pulled up beside the man. A ride was offered, and the hitchhiker accepted. Stories were exchanged, the driver shared the Gospel with his new friend, and a life was changed for eternity. The gentleman who told me about this incident was the hitchhiker, and he was eternally grateful—to the driver and to God.

All God needs is a willing heart. I'm glad he found some willing hearts around me. How about you?

questions to ponder . . .

1. Who has God has used to change your life? How has God changed you through them?

2. Have you thanked God for them? Have you thanked them?

3. How has God used you to change the lives of others?

4. What can you do to make yourself a more effective vessel of God's blessings for others?

time in prayer . . .

Thank God for the opportunity to know him. Thank him for the way he uses the right people at the right time to reveal himself. Ask him to remind you of the people he has used in your life. Pray for those people.

You changed the world

The world is so
big . . . how can
I possibly make
a difference?

■ He said to them, "Go into all the world and
preach the good news to all creation."

Mark 16:15

what can i do?

It's a big world with hundreds of countries, hundreds of languages, and billions of people. But every single person has a story—where they came from, what they've been through, and where they're going. And every individual has needs—food, shelter, clothing, to love, and to be loved. We're all sinners, and we all need a Savior. But the world is so big . . . how can we possibly make a difference?

If we believe the Gospel, odds are that we will want to share it, because it is, after all—the Good News. But how do we reach the world for Christ? How do we share the good news of the Gospel with so many? The way we share the Gospel with a big world is *one person at a time.* God knows us individually. He knit each of us together in our mothers' wombs (Psalm 139). He cares about each and every person, and he loves us so much that he sent his Son to die for each one of us.

If you were the only person on earth, would God have still sent his Son as a sacrifice to save you? Absolutely. Lovingly. Jesus says, "I am the good shepherd. The good shepherd lays down his life for the sheep" (John 10:11). Then Jesus told this parable:

> Suppose one of you has a hundred sheep and loses one of them. Does he not leave the ninety-nine in the open country and go after the lost sheep until he finds it? And when he finds it, he joyfully puts it on his shoulders and goes home. Then he calls his friends and neighbors together and says, "Rejoice with me; I have found my lost sheep." I tell you that in the same way there will be more rejoicing in heaven over one sinner who repents than over ninety-nine righteous persons who do not need to repent. (Luke 15:3–7)

One lost person is important to God. And individuals should also be important to us. What can we do? Where do we start? We can start by loving those around us. We can start by loving the people God places along the paths of our lives. "We love because he first loved us" (1 John 4:19). We can listen to their stories. We can help meet their needs. And we can share the good news of the Gospel and the love of Jesus through our lives as well as our words. Only God can change a heart, but he can use us in the process.

Some people are missionaries in a foreign land—learning, loving, and living in a culture different from their own. Others serve in the inner city. Some feel a burden for the elderly, and others, for children. The world is the mission field, and we are commissioned to take the good news to the corners of the earth—to every nook and cranny. The world may be big, it may seem overwhelming, but it's made up of individuals—people like you and me. And whether we are in a country far from home or in a home down the street, there are people around us with needs. We just need to love them—one person at a time.

questions to ponder . . .

1. Who do you know whose lives you might touch?
2. What are their stories? What are their needs?
3. What would it look like to love them?

time in prayer . . .

Thank God for loving you personally and for sending his Son to die for you. Ask him to help you see the people in your life as individuals and to show you what it means to love them. Ask God to use you, in whatever way he chooses, to reach the world for Christ.